CREATIVITY IN AUTISM

CREATIVITY IN AUTISM

Clare Lawrence and Olivia Macnab

Emerald Guides
www.straightforwardbooks.co.uk

Emerald Guides

© Clare Lawrence and Olivia Macnab 2024

Clare Lawrence and Olivia Macnab have asserted the moral rights to be identified as the author of this work.

All rights reserved. No part of this publication may be reproduced in a retrieval system or transmitted by any means, electronic or mechanical, photocopying or otherwise, without the prior permission of the copyright holders.

British Library Cataloguing in Publication Data. A catalogue record for this book is available from the British Library.

ISBN 978-1-80236-292-3

Printed by 4edge www.4edge.co.uk
Cover artwork by Susanna Matthan Cover design by Catherine Brown
Formatting by Frabjous Books

Whilst every effort has been taken to ensure that the information presented in this book is accurate at the time of going to print, the authors and publishers cannot accept any liability for errors or omissions contained within.

Contents

Foreword by Helen Kara	vii
Acknowledgements	ix
INTRODUCTION	1
1. AUTISTIC ENGLISH TEACHERS AND THE EXPERIENCES OF READING AND WRITING	13
2. THE SHARED READING PROJECT	21
Part One: Shared Reading of the First Verse of Wordsworth's 'Daffidills'	22
Part Two: Beyond words	42
3. CREATIVE WRITING PROJECT	65
4. WHAT HAS EMERGED FROM THESE PROJECTS?	127

Foreword

I am delighted to write a foreword for this book which firmly dispels the myth that autistic people are not, and cannot be, creative. I am a creative autistic person myself, with special interests in creative research methods and creative writing in research, and I have written books on these and other topics. So, this project is close to my heart and each chapter really resonated with me. I particularly appreciated the way the authors apply their learning with a light touch, which makes the book easily readable for lay people as well as academics.

The book includes the perspectives of autistic English teachers, readers, writers, poets, performers, and students, as well as its autistic academic authors. This plurivocality adds richness, and the different voices give intriguing layers of depth to the book's argument and conclusions. Also, this helps to dispel another myth: that autistic people are a homogeneous group. The book takes a social model, difference not deficit approach to autism, and a flexible, open-minded approach to creativity. Plentiful examples demonstrate the creativity of a wide range of autistic people.

I think this book would be useful for you to read if you are:

- An autistic person
- A family member, friend, colleague, or employer of an autistic person
- A researcher or student of autism or neurodiversity
- Someone who is interested in neurodiversity, writing, creativity, and/or different manifestations of humanity.

Thank you for reading this foreword. I hope you enjoy the rest of the book.

Helen Kara
November 2023

Acknowledgements

We are extremely grateful to everyone who has contributed to this exciting and rewarding venture. We offered anonymity to participants throughout – but you know who you are, and we give you our sincere thanks.

We are grateful also to Susanna Matthan for supplying the cover artwork and to Catherine Brown for the cover design.

Introduction

This book reports on two creative projects co-developed by members of the autism community to explore lived experience of autism. For many years in the past autism was seen simply as a disorder, as something that could be identified through perceived deficits which led to a medical diagnosis. Neurotypical doctors observed the behaviour of children (most often, at that time, boys) and labelled what was 'disordered' in these children. Autism was positioned as akin to an illness.

Increasingly, though, as the voice of autistic people has been better heard over the last twenty years and as understanding has developed, this positioning is being revisited.[1] There is a growing movement that suggests that the conventional positioning of autism as a condition defined through medical criteria should be reconsidered. Instead, a lens of neurodiversity may be used, understanding autism as one variation within the many different manifestations of the human condition. Similarly, the term neurodivergent has been adopted by many to identify autism as one way that the brain works differently to the more usual

---

[1] Pellicano, E., & den Houting, J. (2022). Annual Research Review: Shifting from 'normal science' to neurodiversity in autism science. Journal of Child Psychology and Psychiatry, 63(4), 381-396.

(neurotypical). Both terms encompass a range of presentations including autism, ADHD and dyslexia.

This acceptance model positions autism as a difference rather than a deficit. While we, as the writers of this book, prefer this model of understanding, as members of the autism community we also understand the many challenges that autism can bring, and it is this very duality that we explore through our work. Our exploration is into autism as both disabling and empowering, as a difference and as a challenge, as something that can be both preventative and enabling. What is essential to this exploration is that it is undertaken from the inside. We want to re-examine what concepts of autism mean when experienced by real people living in the real world, and to explore autistic people's experiences to articulate the diversity and complexity of that lived experience.

Why creativity?

It can be difficult to describe a difference when that difference for you is the norm. To do so requires the speaker to understand one lived reality and then to describe their own experience as how it counters that. How can an autistic person, for whom being autistic is the only way of being that is known, explain that way of being to someone who is not autistic? How do you identify what is different? How do you explain in a way that is accessible to someone who does not share your experience of the world?

INTRODUCTION

This dilemma has been described as the 'double empathy' problem[2]; autistic people may struggle to instinctively understand the positioning of neurotypical people, but equally neurotypical people may struggle to instinctively understand the autistic perspective. How to overcome this communication barrier is a challenge, and as descriptions of autism include it as being a 'social communication deficit', this suggests a further complication.

One approach to this conundrum may be, we feel, through using creative approaches[3]. These include a whole variety of 'new' ways that knowledge or understanding can be created, and – importantly – are designed to include the realities of the participants in the research. These creative approaches are about the people who are the subject of the research co-creating their own meanings, supported by creative approaches developed and evolved by researchers who are themselves, preferably, from within the group being researched. The concept has evolved not least from Indigenous research methods, where peoples from outside the Euro-Western paradigm conduct research in ways that are firmly embedded in their own culture.[4]

---

[2] Milton, D. E. (2012). On the ontological status of autism: The 'double empathy problem'. Disability & society, 27(6), 883-887.

[3] Ridout, S. (2017). The autistic voice and creative methodologies. Qualitative Research Journal, 17(1), 52-64. See also, for example Teti, M., Cheak-Zamora, N., Lolli, B., & Maurer-Batjer, A. (2016). Reframing autism: Young adults with autism share their strengths through photo-stories. Journal of pediatric nursing, 31(6), 619-629.

[4] Kara, H. (2020). Creative Research Methods 2e: A Practical Guide. Policy Press.

Additionally, it is well-evidenced that creative approaches – particularly those based within written and performed words – can increase empathy and understanding, particularly when expressing the experiences of minority or misunderstood groups.[5] Examples may be found, for example, in the influence of Black playwrights such as debbie tucker green (sic), or feminist writers like Margaret Atwood.[6]

Specifically, given the culture of autism and given the experiences of the two researchers of these projects, we chose to approach our exploration through the medium of creative language. We wanted to explore autism in relation to non-literal language. When autism was first described, it was perceived that autistic people took a literal approach to the world and did not understand metaphor. Even today some diagnostic processes include a lack of understanding of metaphor or non-literal language as part of their criteria. However, recent research is beginning to challenge this idea, and we wish to explore this further.[7] The second reason we

---

[5] Hawkins, L. K., & Certo, J. L. (2014). It's something that I feel like writing, instead of writing because I'm being told to: Elementary boys' experiences writing and performing poetry. Pedagogies: An International Journal, 9(3), 196–215. https://doi.org/10.1080/1554480X.2014.921857

[6] e.g. Grant, A. (2018). debbie tucker green: ear for eye and the Element of Surprise. Arts Foundation Visionary. https://visionaryarts.org.uk/debbie-tucker-green-her-theatrics-and-the-element-of-surprise/

[7] e.g. Kasirer, A., & Mashal, N. (2014). Verbal creativity in autism: Comprehension and generation of metaphoric language in high-functioning autism spectrum disorder and typical development. Frontiers in Human Neuroscience, 8. https://doi.org/10.3389/fnhum.2014.00615

INTRODUCTION

chose this approach was the practical experience of us as researchers, both of whom use language as our primary tool. Clare, an English teacher and university lecturer, works with English graduates just entering the teaching profession. Olivia is a theatre practitioner and writer who uses drama to empower, enfranchise and support a diverse array of communities and experiences through Applied Drama in the Community.

It is also important to note that this emphasis on words must not exclude those autistic people for whom speaking is not a primary or preferred form of communication. When we talk about the 'voice' of autistic people it is essential to be clear that this need not be a spoken voice. Some autistic people are non-speaking, but absence of expressive language should never be taken to assume lack of receptive language, and literature and the written word may very well be a vehicle for rich exploration for those autistic people who do not use spoken words. This subject is explored further through our reading of artefacts rather than words in the second part of the Shared Reading project (Chapter Two). Symbol or metaphor, we believe, should not be overlooked as valuable tools for exploration by all people. The responses to creative language given in this book give some examples of how connections can be made, and so understanding may be shared.

A word about language

As we are discussing language, it is important that we are open about our own language use. The language of autism changes very rapidly. Debates rage around the continued use of the term Asperger syndrome for those initially diagnosed with that label, around person first or identity first language ('person with autism' or 'autistic person'), around the use of less medicalised terminology such as neurodiverse, neurodivergent and neuroqueer. It can be very difficult to get language 'right' in a way that does not hurt or offend, and we are keen to be inclusive and not to alienate any reader by our use of terminology.

After consideration we have chosen to use identity first language and to use the term 'autistic' as our primary term. This generally reflects usage by the participants in these projects and, although it is now some years old, findings by Kenny et al.[8] which asked the wider autism community about preferred terminology. Having said that, we responded throughout this work to the preferences of the people with whom we are working, so other terminology is used at various points. It all adds to the richness!

Who is this book for?

This book is a personal reflection by the writers and reports on our individual and discussed readings and views of the projects we undertook. It cannot and must not be read as 'fact'; it is a reflection on the activities and approaches we used, and most importantly it is a platform for the voice of the autistic people who worked with us to be heard. It is our individual feedback

---

[8] Kenny, L., Hattersley, C., Molins, B., Buckley, C., Povey, C., & Pellicano, E. (2016). Which terms should be used to describe autism? Perspectives from the UK autism community. Autism, 20(4), 442-462.

INTRODUCTION

on the individual perspectives as shared in those activities. All autistic people are different, and this can only ever be an example of what some autistic people have said at some times.

However, wider understanding of autism is vastly enriched by inclusion of the voice of autistic people. If autism is to be understood, it is the experience of autism from the autistic perspective that is going to facilitate that understanding. Although one perspective of one autistic person can (and should) not be generalised, each individual perspective of each individual autistic person is nevertheless extremely valuable. Additionally, the breadth of real autistic voices in current research is limited and historically an insider perspective has focussed on that of the parents of autistic children and young people. We hope to encourage the diversity and volume of autistic voices by amplifying those that we have been able to work with, as well as our own.

Some readers may be interested to follow up on the academic work that underpins this book. To that end we give footnotes to lead to some examples or sample research as a starting point for that exploration. Again, this is not exhaustive but should, we hope, provide signposting to some of the richness of autistic discussion that is available.

Who are we?

Clare is an Associate Professor working in the field of Participatory Autism Research. Her interest is in capturing autistic experience from within the autism community – autistic people, together with parents, friends, partners and teachers in the many ways that these identities merge and overlap. She was, for example, one of the first researchers to explore the perspective of autistic teachers and is particularly interested in autistic perspectives on literature. Her son received a formal diagnosis of autism in 2002 at the age of four, when autism was still viewed very strongly as a 'disability'. As she has watched him grow and thrive, her understanding has developed and she is proud to feel that, as an autistic researcher and writer herself, she has contributed in some small part to the quantum shift in perceptions of autism away from seeing it as a medical condition and towards it being a different human presentation.

Olivia is a writer and Applied Drama practitioner. They specialise in using theatre techniques with different communities in order to empower people, encourage community development and empower people to have a platform for their voices to be heard. Applied Drama has a rich history, and discussion of its techniques and understanding is presented in more detail in Chapter Three. Olivia is an autistic practitioner who began to truly explore their autistic experience while at university and has often used their research and projects to explore the application of Applied Drama with the autism community. They first began an interest in Applied Drama after volunteering with a sensory drama group for adults living with learning difficulties and hope to continue specialising in working with similar groups as they develop their own full-time freelance portfolio. Theatre and creative writing have always been a safe space for them, and a medium through which they can express themselves and make their voice heard in a world which so often seemed to misunderstand them at best; and they hope to provide that opportunity for others throughout their creative practice.

The projects and the structure of this book

Chapter One reproduces an article first published in the National Association for Teachers of English magazine *Teaching English* which gives voice to some autistic English teachers regarding their perspectives on reading and writing. The perspective of autistic teachers remains under-heard, although research interest is growing.[9] Hearing from autistic people who are highly articulate and knowledgeable about language and the written word, about their own experience of it and how that impacts their teaching of it, gives a perspective that is an important starting point for this book. How might an autistic person read a poem or a book differently? How might autism impact the creative writing process?[10]

Chapter Two specifically explores reading and discussion, in other words the process of making meaning from words,

---

[9] Wood, R., & Happé, F. (2023). What are the views and experiences of autistic teachers? Findings from an online survey in the UK. Disability & society, 38(1), 47-72 Wood, R. (2023). Happier on the outside? Discourses of exclusion, disempowerment and belonging from former autistic school staff. Journal of Research in Special Educational Needs.

[10] See also Finn-Kelcey, I. (2021). To what extent does the 'Double Empathy Problem' impact on the assessment and grading of autistic students' creative writing?. Good Autism Practice (GAP), 22(1), 24-37.

images or objects. The methodology behind the project is that of Shared Reading, an approach pioneered by the charity The Reader[11] where literature is read aloud and members of the group are encouraged by the group leader to respond by making connections, sharing memories and discussing experiences prompted by the text. The reading aloud of the literature is an essential component. Voicing of poetry, and the hearing of it in your own and others' voices, is an important element that is becoming less common in the classroom and in society.[12] In earlier times literature was read aloud as a social activity, and this brings with it an immediacy that silent, private reading does not. It allows the words to be experienced in 'real time', with each person hearing those words simultaneously so that there is an association and relatedness to the group experience from the outset.

In this case the group members were autistic adults, parents of autistic children and those who were both. The projects, as discussed in an academic article in *Good Autism Practice*[13] ran for two sessions, each of six weeks, and explored in total 12 different examples of literature. The feedback was so rich and abundant that in order for the approach to be fully critiqued in this book, the comments on just a single verse of one poem

---

[11] Home – The Reader | Shared Reading groups at Calderstones and beyond

[12] Alexander, J. (2022). The Newbolt Report and reading aloud: an overview of the emergence and subsequent development of a poetry pedagogy. English in Education, 56(1), 59-72.

[13] Lawrence, C. (2022). Dancing with the daffodils: using a Shared Reading approach to explore autistic identity. Good Autism Practice (GAP), 23(1), 5-13.

INTRODUCTION

are discussed. This is the group's responses to the first verse of William Wordsworth's poem, 'I wandered lonely as a cloud'.

The project also involved an adaptation of the approach in that it sought to move away from a sole focus on words. Some autistic people do not use spoken language, and this pilot approach supplemented the literature with objects, chosen by the participant, with the invitation to 'read' what they might mean for autism. These discussions followed the same format as for the Shared Reading of literature, in that they took place in the group with the group leader hosting the discussion. However, two further examples emerged at the end of the project when we received two typed contributions. Although still at an early stage, the use of objects or 'artefacts' as a vehicle for expressions of autistic experience away from spoken words and discussion forms an exciting development in research.

Chapter Three reports on a creative writing and theatre project developed with a group of neurodivergent students. The group utilised a participatory approach to creative writing, developing what emerged into a theatrical performance. Perspectives on autism, identity and the student experience were explored. Over the course of the project, participants developed a number of pieces of poetry, prose and script based on proposed prompts, intended to bring out aspects of their lived experience. They then selected some of their pieces to enter into an anthology, and of those pieces, narrowed it down further to select some pieces to be performed for an audience.

The project took place across twelve weeks, with three sessions taking place every week, and was split into three sections: Writing, Editing and Performing. There were also some additional sessions developed in association with an on-campus mental wellbeing project known as Wellbeing Wednesdays. The group consisted of both undergraduate and post-graduate students, and a wide range of pieces was produced displaying a diverse array of experiences.

The chapter begins by exploring the theory, processes and inspirations behind the project, giving the reader an understanding of Applied Drama and its methodologies, and the initial research that took place. It follows with an exploration of the process used throughout the project and the inner workings of the practice. Finally, the prompts used throughout the project are explored, with examples provided from the anthology and discussion shared regarding their meanings and the inspirations involved in their development.

Finally, Chapter Four summarises themes that have emerged from these projects and explores what they might tell us about creativity in autism and about the lived experience of autism as experienced by these volunteers.

**

CHAPTER 1

Autistic English Teachers and the Experiences of Reading and Writing

This chapter was first published in the National Association for Teachers of English (NATE) Secondary Magazine, Teaching English[14]*. We are grateful to the editors for permission to include it here. The projects discussed in this book use reading, writing and discussion as their primary tools. These elements are the traditional remit of subject English in schools – so it seems a good starting point to explore autism (and the use of these elements of subject English) from the perspective of those autistic people who work as English teachers.*

As an Initial Teacher Education lecturer, I am privileged to be able to support autistic trainee teachers on their PGCE journeys. This statement still seems to surprise some people. For some, the

---

[14] Lawrence, C. (2022). "Was it a cat I saw?": working with autistic English teachers to support understanding of our pupils' autism perspectives. Teaching English.

perception is that autism remains something that affects pupils, and it is for we the adults to 'support' or 'make adjustments for' these children. But we know that autistic children grow up into autistic adults, and it really should surprise no one that some of these adults choose to become teachers.

Nor are these teachers constrained within the traditional, stereotyped subjects. Yes, we do have autistic maths and physics trainees, but we also have autistic students learning to be art teachers, music teachers, geography teachers and – most certainly – English teachers.

It has been a huge pleasure for me to work with a number of these autistic English trainee teachers as they have made their successful journey to Qualified Teacher Status (QTS) over the past few years. The insights that they have brought have hugely enriched all of our journeys. Of course, all autistic people are different, and each autistic teacher can only give one perspective on the world of education. However, I believe this perspective remains hugely important, not least because understanding of autism in schools remains distressingly poor. Again and again when I visit classrooms to observe my trainees teach I am told by the mentor or usual class teacher that an autistic pupil in that class is 'fine'. In a sense I am happy to believe them – I have known a great many very fine autistic people – but unfortunately that is not what is meant. Too often teachers still judge the well being of autistic pupils through behaviour: if the pupil is quiet and compliant, the assumption is that all is well (or it is even suggested that the identification is in error

1. AUTISTIC ENGLISH TEACHERS

and the pupil is not in fact autistic). Yet we know that autism is not behaviour, and we know also that autism carries with it differences and challenges in communication. I am left to wonder how a neurotypical teacher makes the assessment that an autistic pupil is 'fine' if they are judging wholly on their own neurotypical communication criteria.

So how might we begin to understand how autism interacts with the experience of studying English? The autistic English teachers I have known have shared so many nuanced insights into a different way of thinking and interacting with the world and with subject English. The twelve short examples given below give, I believe, a flavour of their perspectives and, as such, some small windows into the experience of the subject of English from an autistic perspective.

> "I enjoy literature of course, but I can find some imagery overwhelming. For example (and I hate describing this!), the reference to men without boots limping 'blood-shod' in *Dulce et Decorum Est* is almost too painful to process. The sensory power of the blood mixing with the mud – the colours, the germs, the pain, the cold, the awful sensitivity of feet – is overwhelming. I have come to dread teaching the poem as I find that image, that one in particular, stays with me and unsettles me for the rest of the day."

> "My passion is for grammar and I can scarcely contain myself when we are analysing a piece of literature. I

have to control my urge to deconstruct every sentence, identifying every part of speech and linguistic technique and ruminating on the precise reason the writer chose *that* word or *that* order. The children know this and ask me questions to 'get me started'. But my pupils are always pretty strong on language analysis!"

"Sometimes I find fiction very frustrating. I mean, why doesn't King Lear simply go home? He's divided his kingdom and his residency between his daughters, but his original castle must still be there. All that roaming about on the moor seems unnecessary to me."

"The word 'spring' was used in a poem that I was sharing with the class, meaning the season that precedes summer. I read it the first time as being a spring as in a coil, and I couldn't get that out of my head. It was like I was looking at two poems simultaneously, one about a season and one about hardware."

"I really struggle with embarrassment, and cringe-worthy moments. I hate the whole Malvolio thing in *Twelfth Night*. Bullying isn't funny."

"The trouble is that I see my autistic son in each of my autistic pupils, and I know how upset he gets if I say I'll read him a chapter for his bedtime story and then I can't. I hate it when something happens in class, and I can't read the bit of the book that I've said we'll be

1. AUTISTIC ENGLISH TEACHERS

covering. Most of the kids don't care but I know I'm letting down my autistic pupils, and I should be better than that."

"I spent a wonderful Saturday afternoon after reading Celia's article (Lawrence et al., 2021[15]), looking at the different uses of 'sit' and 'set' in *Of Mice and Men*. I found that 'sit' (or 'sitting') appears eleven times in the novella, and 'set' – meaning to sit – 23 times. As Celia says, Steinbeck allows the words to imply subtly different conditions. For example, Crooks asks Lennie to 'set down' (p. 69) and join him, yet when he goes on to describe his lonely life he asks Lennie to imagine, 'S'pose you had to sit out here an' read books' (p. 72). To 'set' is to settle, where 'sit' feels uncomfortable. Marvellous!"

"Books are not real life and we should be careful not to set them out to be. For example, I'm quite like Mr Darcy; I am tall and quiet and socially awkward. Does that make me 'sexy'? I don't think so. (Granted, I do not own a large estate in Derbyshire.)"

"My sense of humour at school gets me into trouble. I love palindromes ('Was it a cat I saw?') and puns. I get hung up on kennings and I can hear myself

---

[15] Lawrence, C* C., Collyer, E., & Poulson, M. (2021). "Howling at the scrabble-board": exploring classroom literature from an autistic viewpoint. English in Education, 55(2), 164-176.

banging on about them even when I know my pupils haven't the faintest idea what I'm talking about. Is being 'funny' a good thing in a teacher?"

"I've always enjoyed re-reading texts and will read the same books again and again to relax. One of the great things now that I am qualified is that I'm teaching the same texts this year as I did last. I'm finding new things to highlight because of the responses pupils made last time. I can feel my enjoyment growing and my teaching getting richer with each cycle."

"I can't bear injustice. The events in *Atonement* make me feel physically sick. I even struggle with the policeman's tricks in *An Inspector Calls*. It's all very clever, but at the end of the day he is lying and is deceiving the family, and that is wrong."

"I get enthusiastic about things, and that has always meant a real passion for elements of English. We were taken to a production of *Hamlet* when I was doing my A levels, and it just 'blew me away'. I went back to see that production again and again. I must have seen it ten times. I could quote great swathes of it. I discovered John Dover Wilson's 1951 book *What Happens in Hamlet* in the library and read it repeatedly.

Sadly, the set text for the exam that year was *The Tempest*!

1. AUTISTIC ENGLISH TEACHERS

What these snippets from autistic English teachers show us is that autistic people may be focussing on elements that are just a little different to those of the rest of the class. They may be hyper focused on one element, may be struggling to maintain an overview of the whole, may be repulsed or distressed by a particular image, event or word use. Conversely, they may be enjoying literature in a way that others have missed or be engrossed in a particular element. The teachers who share these examples have all graduated as being 'good' at English, so have found ways of decoding the implications of non-verbal cues in texts. Indeed, one told me that he learned to understand back and forth dialogue through reading examples in novels, and another that she hadn't understood how a look or a gesture could carry meaning until Jane Austen showed her. However, this may not yet be true for some autistic pupils and they – even the brightest of them – may 'trip up' on what may seem quite simple points. The uneven profile of autism has both peaks and troughs, and I believe that it is essential that teachers are alert for both, for the variation in teaching that may be required and for the potential for originality and insight that autism may bring to our classrooms.

**

CHAPTER 2

The Shared Reading Project

Clare Lawrence

This chapter reports on the responses of participants taking part in Shared Reading of a verse from a poem, and of objects or artefacts. These are used as scaffolds to discuss their experiences of autism. The people taking part were autistic adults, parents of autistic children and those who were both. Initially, these descriptors were seen as separate, but many of the autistic adults taking part were also parents of autistic children, and all the parents of autistic children identified as autistic. Ages ranged from early twenties to mid-sixties. What all members – and the group leader – shared was an interest in autism and a desire to articulate their lived experiences.

PART ONE
SHARED READING OF THE FIRST VERSE OF WORDSWORTH'S 'DAFFODILS'

The initial part of the Shared Reading project focussed, as traditionally recommended by the method, on 'serious literature'. Although difficult to define, in this case serious literature is taken to refer to writing that engages with significant human situations[16] and in which the words, phrases or lexicon have a conscious intention by the writer.[17] The assumption with a segment of poetry as discussed here is that the writer has chosen his words with care, that he decided consciously on their order and their form, the way they sound and the way they work with each other. It is assumed that he wrote what he wrote for a reason, not idly but intentionally. Although we as readers may not share that intention, nor even recognise it, the fact that the verse was created attentively gives potential – we hope – for it to resonate with us and to prompt reactions and connections.

> **'I wandered lonely as a cloud'**
>
> *by William Wordsworth*
>
> I wandered lonely as a cloud
> That floats on high o'er vales and hills,

---

[16] For example, Davis, P. (2013). Reading and the reader: The literary agenda. Literary Agenda.

[17] Pater, W. (1888). Style. Fortnightly, 44(264), 728-743.

2. THE SHARED READING PROJECT

> When all at once I saw a crowd,
> A host, of golden daffodils;
> Beside the lake, beneath the trees,
> Fluttering and dancing in the breeze.

Before reading further we suggest that you pause here and take time to consider this verse. Read it aloud more than once and think about what images and ideas it provokes. Can you 'see' the daffodils in your mind's eye? Do you experience any other sensations, the rustling of the trees, for example, or the movement of the breeze against your skin? Can you recall a time when you just stood and stared, and what memories does this evoke? Is there anything in these short lines that makes you think of elements in your own life, or are there particular words or phrases that you find make connections with your experiences?

Participants' responses

The initial barrier that I faced when I started this project was the participants' proclaimed dislike of poetry. There was a real hostility to it, that poetry is "wordy", that it "doesn't say what it means" and that the members of the group felt that "we just don't get it". This attitude may be a response due to autism, but I suspect that it is not. In my role as a teacher-educator supporting graduates to become qualified English teachers, I have talked to a huge range of English teachers and prospective English teachers. It never ceases to amaze me how few of them profess a love of poetry. Poetry, more than any other literary form, seems to have been damaged by the analytical approaches to literature demanded by elements of our current examination system[18]. In so many ways, poetry is viewed with suspicion.

Wandering

My first task, then, was to find a way for the group members to begin to engage with the poem. Experience (of myself and others) suggests that merely directing an autistic person to 'pay attention' is unlikely to result in success. Instead, the advantage of autistic focus needs to be brought to bear. Autistic focus has an intensity, an immersive quality and an ability to make connections which is one of the joys of autism.[19] All the group members were present because of an interest in autism, specifically in their own lived experience of it. There was a shared desire to articulate autistic perspective, so that the challenge was to support the members to see the poem as a vehicle for this articulation. With this in mind I initially read the whole poem aloud and then we focussed on the first verse, various group members reading it aloud again so that it could resonate from different voices. We also allowed plenty of 'space' for the words to register and for the members of the group to begin to make connections.

---

[18] For a discussion on the way poetry teaching has evolved, see Blake, J. (2020). What did the National Curriculum do for poetry (Doctoral dissertation, PhD thesis, University of Cambridge).

[19] Murray, D. (2018). Monotropism—an interest based account of autism. Encyclopedia of autism spectrum disorders, 10, 978-981.

2. THE SHARED READING PROJECT

To begin, I encouraged the group members to volunteer something – anything – that they liked about the verse. Eventually, and somewhat tentatively, one member suggested that he liked the idea of 'wandering'. When pushed to explain in more detail he said that he liked the idea of the poet not knowing where he was going, of just drifting and following whatever path he wanted. He also liked the idea of allowing your thoughts to 'wander', to link to memories, make connections and to follow their own path. We talked about this for some time as this approach was exactly the attitude needed for the Shared Reading activity. The purpose of the sessions was for the members to allow their ideas to 'wander', to follow thoughts about autism and memories of different experiences as they happened, and not to worry about any concept of there being a 'right' answer. The purpose of the group was most definitely not poetry analysis, but to use the poem as a springboard, a stepping off point to explore various experiences of autism. Gradually, with this attitude in mind, the responses started to come – and how rich they were!

"Lonely as a cloud"

This simile was the first phrase to really 'grab' the discussion, and we talked about why a cloud might be perceived as lonely. The image of the cloud, we felt, was often negative. We discussed the drawing of a cloud over a person's head to suggest that they are depressed, and sayings such as 'every cloud has a silver lining' that position the cloud as – even when containing something positive – being initially conceived as something unwanted.

Clouds bring rain, they can block the sun, they are dark. This concept, coupled with that of loneliness, seemed to us to be a wholly unhappy, even frightening image.

However, thinking further we wondered why this particular cloud might be described as 'lonely'. We concluded that this would only be the case on a fine day, when a blue sky might be dotted with one or two small, fluffy clouds drifting gently along – 'floating'. These clouds are not threatening and are not seen as marring the beauty of the day. We were confident that in the way the image is being presented in this verse it was a positive image, and we then discussed the word 'lonely' in that context.

Many of us felt that we have been lonely at various points in our lives and some of the parents expressed concern that their autistic children might be lonely. Additionally, we identified that we are sometimes seen as lonely by others even when we are not. There was a confidence expressed that to be alone is not automatically to be lonely. Members stated their pleasure in being alone, indeed their need to be alone at times to 'reset' or self-repair. There was a discussion that the concept of 'lonely' is in some ways a neurotypical one when referring to autism. Many were keen to express that aloneness, if understood as self-reliance, can be a good thing, and we felt that we are often encouraged or forced into social activities when we would far prefer to be alone. One member suggested that the cloud adds beauty to a blue sky. Without the cloud there is little perspective on the infinite blueness, and the cloud in fact enhances the fineness of the day. We agreed that Wordsworth's description of

2. THE SHARED READING PROJECT

the cloud was a good metaphor for autistic isolation, especially as one cloud of this type is seldom, actually, alone; if there is one white cloud in an otherwise blue sky there is every chance that there will be some more somewhere. We discussed the feeling of community that recognition of autism can bring, how there can be companionship and support in recognising kinship with other neurodiverse people. All members expressed that they are happier now that they understand that they are autistic, and that knowing yourself also gives you permission to be yourself – to be alone if you want to be and not to feel forced to be part of the neurotypical crowd.

We concluded that the concept of 'loneliness' in autism[20] is one that is interesting and is well worth considering further, especially from within the autism community.

"I love daffodils because I love red and green together."

This comment when made by one of the group members astonished and delighted us all. The rest of us all said that the colour we 'see' at the word daffodil is overwhelmingly yellow, with perhaps some gold or orange, although we agreed that some

---

[20] For example, Deckers, A., Muris, P., & Roelofs, J. (2017). Being on your own or feeling lonely? Loneliness and other social variables in youths with autism spectrum disorders. Child Psychiatry & Human Development, 48, 828-839; Umagami, K., Remington, A., Lloyd-Evans, B., Davies, J., & Crane, L. (2022). Loneliness in autistic adults: A systematic review. Autism, 26(8), 2117-2135; Quadt, L., Williams, G., Mulcahy, J. S., Silva, M., Larsson, D., Arnold, A.,& Garfinkel, S. (2021). "I'm trying to reach out, I'm trying to find my people" Loneliness and loneliness distress in autistic adults.

daffodils (one mentioned the Red Devon variety) have a centre that approaches red for us all. We also accepted that the green of the leaves and the stalk is an intrinsic element and should not be overlooked. What excited us was that even a common image such as the daffodil can be so different in the 'mind's eye' of different people, and that this may be especially so in autism.

We know that one characteristic of autism is a difference in sensory processing. Messages from the senses – sight, sound, touch, smell, taste, as well as balance and reading of how a person 'feels' inside – may be more or less intense than that experienced by non-autistic individuals. The diagnostic criteria for autism spectrum disorder as defined in the DSM-5[21] includes reference to 'hyper- or hypo-reactivity to sensory input or unusual interest in sensory aspects of the environment'. This group member's enthusiasm for red and green as prompted by thoughts of daffodils is a fine lived example of this. It seems that we do not all occupy the same world as it reaches us through our senses. One has only to look at the detailed and wonderful artwork of Stephen Wiltshire[22] to appreciate that what he sees, and what he retains when he looks, is not the same as that of most people. He can look at a building or cityscape and reproduce it from memory with astonishing accuracy. Clearly, his 'looking' does not include the same qualitative experience as for most other people, yet it is only because he can draw that we know this. How many more autistic people – especially

---

[21] The Diagnostic and Statistical Manual of Mental Disorders, Fifth Edition.

[22] Stephen Wiltshire | Contemporary Artist & Architectural Illustrator

2. THE SHARED READING PROJECT

those who cannot draw or do not use language as their primary form of communication – might 'look' with just such intensity, yet be unable to share that through output?

Nor is the comment regarding the red and green of the daffodils unsupported through medical model autism research. Several papers[23] have commented on autistic people's different processing of colours and on differences of colour vision in autism. It may be that autistic sensory processing does not just make colours more or less intense but may render the experience of those colours in a less usual way for autistic people. Many autistic people find certain colours distressing or overwhelming, or equally find others stimulating or comforting. Understanding how sensory processing works for the individual, and how that alters across the lifetime, in different situations and emotional states, is, we felt, an important part of autism acceptance.

We also discussed the enthusiasm of the speaker, who "loves" daffodils and red and green together. Even when discussing colour perception, research positionality can tend to identify

---

[23] For example, Zachi, E. C., Costa, T. L., Barboni, M. T., Costa, M. F., Bonci, D. M., & Ventura, D. F. (2017). Color vision losses in autism spectrum disorders. Frontiers in psychology, 8, 1127; Maule, J., Skelton, A. E., & Franklin, A. (2023). The development of color perception and cognition. Annual Review of Psychology, 74, 87-111.; Franklin, A., Sowden, P., Burley, R., Notman, L., & Alder, E. (2008). Color perception in children with autism. Journal of autism and developmental disorders, 38(10), 1837-1847; Shareef, S. S., & Farivarsadri, G. (2019). The impact of colour and light on children with autism in interior spaces from an architectural point of view. International Journal of Arts and Technology, 11(2), 153-164.

what colours may be negative for autistic people or may emphasise how certain colours placed together can lead to visual distortion or overload. The joy of these two colours juxtaposed is supported by proponents of Colour Theories[24] who suggest that philosophically and scientifically as well as artistically, colours matter. We discussed how it may be that autistic focus and potential heightened sensory awareness may mean that colours are experienced and can be enjoyed more intensely in autism. If nothing else, the speaker's enthusiasm means that Christmas, with its emphasis on the colours of red and green, is a particularly happy time for her!

"The daffodils make me think of my son walking on tiptoe and 'flapping'".

The daffodils are described as 'fluttering and dancing', and for one autistic father of an autistic son this brought the image of his young son's movements to mind.

As the literature on autism confirms,[25] repetitive movements and motor differences are a common element of autism and

---

[24] For example, Roque, G. (2023). Colour theory: Definition, fields and interrelations. Journal of the International Colour Association, 32, 4-16.

[25] For example, Valagussa, G., Purpura, G., Nale, A., Pirovano, R., Mazzucchelli, M., Grossi, E., & Perin, C. (2022). Sensory Profile of Children and Adolescents with Autism Spectrum Disorder and Tip-Toe Behavior: Results of an Observational Pilot Study. Children, 9(9), 1336.; Lakkapragada, A., Kline, A., Mutlu, O. C., Paskov, K., Chrisman, B., Stockham, N., ... & Wall, D. P. (2022). The classification of abnormal hand movement to aid in autism detection: Machine learning study. JMIR Biomedical Engineering, 7(1), e33771.

observed 'stereotyped' movements are used as part of current diagnostic criteria. The father's connection between his son's movements and those of the daffodils, however, was entirely positive. He confirms that his son's movements are as often an expression of excitement or joy as of distress, and that he values them as a form of communication. There is a naturalness in the description of the daffodils that we all agreed to be positively reflected in autistic gestures, suggesting a spontaneity and lack of inhibition in expression.

Among the group, though, we all agreed that we tend to supress these gestures in ourselves – at least in public – and also that we struggle not to supress the behaviours in our autistic children. "Standing out", "looking different", "acting autistic" were all reasons given why we worried about these natural expressions of communication, and this led to a detailed and rather sombre discussion. On one hand we all appreciated these gestures and movements as being purposeful as relaxing and self-soothing for ourselves, and also as valid and useful as means of communication with our children … and yet, we all struggled not to control or mask them. We talked about the use of Applied Behavioural Analysis (ABA)[26] as a 'treatment' for autism, which systematically aims to eliminate these kinds of behaviours, and how we felt this approach to be abusive and even dangerous.

---

[26] See Callahan, M. M., Fodstad, J. C., & Moore, J. W. (2023). History of Applied Behavior Analysis. In Handbook of Applied Behavior Analysis: Integrating Research into Practice (pp. 3-17). Cham: Springer International Publishing.

The book *Loud Hands: Autistic People Speaking*[27] was discussed, and how the title was taken as a refutation of the common constraint laid on autistic children to have 'quiet hands' and not to flap or gesture. Recent research[28] has suggested that autistic adults confirm that repetitive behaviours of this kind can help with functionality, reducing otherwise overwhelming stimuli and helping to manage stress. We felt an element of guilt in the way that we supress these behaviours in ourselves and in our children and accepted that it is a problematic conceptualisation of autism to feel a need to modify these behaviours. However, we also acknowledged the stigma that autistic behaviours can carry in the 'real' world. We felt that we are not yet in a place as a society to accept overtly autistic behaviours, and – much though we love the description of the daffodils in all their uninhibited and unselfconscious dancing – we are sadly not yet able to embrace such a freedom for ourselves or for our children.

"The daffodils are all together in a crowd. They are like neurotypical people, dancing all together."

In complete contrast to the idea above, another participant viewed the daffodils as being "like neurotypical people", and this idea was energetically endorsed by other members. The 'otherness' of the daffodils appealed, as did the description

---

[27] Network, A. S. A. (2012). Loud hands: Autistic people, speaking. Autistic Press.

[28] Manor-Binyamini, I., & Schreiber-Divon, M. (2019). Repetitive behaviors: Listening to the voice of people with high-functioning autism spectrum disorder. Research in Autism Spectrum Disorders, 64, 23-30.

of them as a 'crowd'. There was something of a feeling of amusement about the neurotypical daffodil host, perhaps a reaction to the patronisation that many members felt they regularly get from non-autistic people. Descriptors of autism as being a 'deficit' in social interaction, or in developing, maintaining or understanding relationships, were countered in the group's contempt for this neurotypical behaviour. The daffodils are tethered, all crushed in together, moving at the whim of the breeze without autonomy or free choice, and this was felt to be a good analogy for some neurotypical behaviours.

Members mentioned crowded dance floors, or the huge crowds at music or sporting events, and what an anathema such situations are to them. They confirmed with each other how expectations to be involved in situations such as these were a major source of anxiety, citing school or university socialising specifically as being highly challenging, a report endorsed by research.[29]

However, the response went further than a mere easy rejection of such non-autistic behaviour. What further interested the group was the extent to which the poet derived intense pleasure from the daffodils, from their number and from their beauty, but had no wish to go in amongst them. Indeed, it is clear that he has no wish to become a daffodil! As one group member

---

[29] Goddard, H., & Cook, A. (2022). "I spent most of freshers in my Room"– A qualitative study of the social experiences of university students on the autistic spectrum. Journal of Autism and Developmental Disorders, 52(6), 2701-2716.

suggested, "He is gazing in from the outside and won't join in. But he is still getting pleasure from watching and being a part, apart." This statement – especially that concept of being *a part of* even when *apart from* social activities, resonated with the group who articulated how they get social enjoyment from being around people even as they prefer not to become too involved. One gave the example of enjoying the fireworks of new year from the privacy of her garden, knowing that parties are going on all around, having no wish to attend one but still feeling a sense of belonging at the shared event. Another added his excitement about large and busy Gaming Conventions. He has no wish to be there but is happy to join online and to know that other people are there: he enjoys the vicarious 'buzz'. In all, the group agreed that the poet sees the daffodils as beautiful in their large numbers, moving and turning in the wind, and they can see something of that beauty in large groups of people who are enjoying themselves … they just would prefer not to have to 'go in among them'!

The writer is giving a running commentary of what he is doing, narrating his life.

This observation by one member of the group really struck a chord. The members agreed how they will give a commentary of what they are doing in their heads, some indicating that this was their usual way of being whilst others suggested that it was something that they did more in times of stress. What all agreed on was the "joy of monologuing", imparting information about a favourite subject with no desire for any particular response from the recipient of this monologue. There was some discussion as to whether there was actually any need for another person to be there for the commentary to be satisfying. Most members suggested that it was, and the parents of autistic children suggested that, although their children seemed quite happy to commentate on what interested them or what they were doing without an audience, there did seem to be a particular pleasure in the giving of information *to* someone, even when that person took no further part. The parents confessed to sometimes 'switching off' when their children started on these accounts, but also expressed pleasure in the fact that their children wanted to share their interests with them.

Autistic monologuing has been much observed in research from the early days of Kanner's first work on autism to, for example, Rowland's succinct description in 2020:

> 'Autistic people excel at one-way communication. Monologues are our preferred form of oral presentation. We start at square one and create a complete picture of everything we know on a given topic.'[30]

Frequently in the medical literature this is discussed in terms of how to move the autistic person – usually a child or an adult who is being treated like one – away from monologue towards dialogue. The group members did not refute the value of 'back

---

[30] Rowland, D. (2020). How the autistic mind functions – An Insider's Report. Journal of Neurology, Psychiatry and Brain Research, 3. – p. 5

and forth' conversation in addition, but remained adamant that the joy of autistic monologue is more than an inability to interact. We agreed that the ideal job for an autistic person might well be university lecturer, which gives status to the task of talking about your subject with only the most minimal interference from the audience!

It is interesting that DSM-5 identifies an element of autism as being a '...Failure of normal back-and-forth conversation', yet at the same time suggests that autism includes '...reduced sharing of interests'[31] It seems the American Psychiatric Association struggles with the concept that autistic monologuing *is* a form of sharing of interests. Nor does the fact that the monologue requires no immediate response necessarily exclude interaction of a kind. Reader Response Theory[32] suggests that the reader has as important a role in meaning-making of a text as the writer, and that in effect the writer and reader are in a form of dialogue, even while separated by geography and time. This chimes powerfully with the methodology used in this project, but it also has an unforeseen relevance regarding the group's comments about monologuing in autism. As one member remarked, "Why is it okay when the poet does it, but not okay for us?" No one, as far as I am aware, has ever chastised Wordsworth for his one-way description of the daffodils; he saw them, he wrote

---

[31] The Diagnostic and Statistical Manual of Mental Disorders, Fifth Edition.

[32] For example, Davis, J. R. (1992). Reconsidering readers: Louise Rosenblatt and reader-response pedagogy. Research and Teaching in Developmental Education, 8(2), 71-81.

about them in the poem ... and it is for the reader of that poem to make meaning out of his words (i.e., to be in dialogue with him). The group members felt that it was unfortunate, and in no small part unfair, that their joy in the one-way description of what interested them should be seen as a deficit, whereas in Wordsworth it is acceptable and even laudable. We agreed that we must accept perhaps that what constitutes value, art and poetry is in large part driven by (neurotypical) societal principles.

Experiencing the value of something that others might not have noticed.

However, the previous point moved the group on to make this last element of their response to the verse. Presumably, one of the reasons the poem is important is because Wordsworth noticed the daffodils and saw beauty and interest in something that others may not have appreciated. One of the 'deficits' of autism, we are told, is that autistic people have '...interests that are abnormal in intensity or focus'[33] Could Wordsworth's interest in the daffodils be described, in his time, as 'abnormal'? He certainly shows an intensity of interest in them and a focus on them that may have seemed surprising to some at the beginning of the 19th Century.

One of the group shared an experience of his own:

---

[33] The Diagnostic and Statistical Manual of Mental Disorders, Fifth Edition.

CREATIVITY IN AUTISM

> "I was late to a meeting today because I saw a spider shedding its exoskeleton. I noticed that it seemed to have more than eight legs, then I realised what it was doing. It was still pale and damp. I stayed to watch and to take a picture."

He shared the photograph with us, and it was, indeed, both interesting and beautiful. Yet how many non-autistic people would have prioritised the experience over punctuality? And how soon might these relative values need to be revisited for this person if, against the tide of usual autistic experience, he is to succeed in employment?

Autistic focus and attention to detail can be a tremendous asset, and the world we live in can be a source of wonder lost by the 'bigger picture' view of the predominant neurotype. Details matter; focus on minutiae can be a strength. Noticing and taking note of things that pass others by can lead to anything from great art to life-saving safety awareness. The members of the group were happy to share their joy in this aspect of their autistic experience and felt no need to apologise for it nor to seek to desensitise themselves to it. Where many cases of 'support' suggested for autistic people, both for children and adults, involve shift of focus and attention to what the support-giver believes to be important, the group members were confident that their view of the world has a value that needs no remediation.

2. THE SHARED READING PROJECT

Summary of responses to this verse

This Shared Reading approach to the verse yielded rich conversations, and all the participants expressed their valuing of it as an approach, confirming that they found it a helpful scaffold to discuss autism. The methodology has since been used and critiqued in other studies[34] and has been acknowledged to be an interesting and valuable addition to the toolkit for unlocking our understanding of the experience of autism. Using it in this project with reference to just one short verse from one poem, the participants explored a whole host of topics within autism.

- We discussed loneliness, and how being 'lonely as a cloud' could be seen as an autism-appropriate expression for being alone.
- We considered the world of colour as it is perceived and enjoyed by autistic people, and how that is simply one element of a richness of sensory experience which may be different for autistic people both qualitatively and in intensity.
- We discussed naturalness, freedom of expression and how this aligns to the Disability Rights movement. Should autistic people be asked to mask behaviours that serve

---

[34] Chapple, M., Davis, P., Billington, J., & Corcoran, R. (2023). Exploring the different cognitive, emotional and imaginative experiences of autistic and non-autistic adult readers when contemplating serious literature as compared to non-fiction. Frontiers in psychology, 14, 1001268; Chapple, M., Davis, P., Billington, J., Williams, S., & Corcoran, R. (2022). Challenging empathic deficit models of autism through responses to serious literature. Frontiers in Psychology, 13, 828603.

a useful function to them? Should we/do we mask our own behaviours and how should we discuss this issue with our children? Does anyone have a right to close down this form of expression and communication when it is doing no harm to others?

- We thought of the daffodils as a crowd of people all together and moving as one, and used that as a way to discuss the differences in social interaction that can exist between autistic and non-autistic people. We discussed in particular the appeal of being a part of a group whilst remaining apart from it.
- We talked about the joy of monologuing, and wondered at why it is shut down by those who seek to alter autistic behaviours. We reflected on what 'dialogue' is, how it can occur across time and space when happening between a writer and a reader, and how our 'monologues' could be seen as dialogue that is simply presented differently.
- Finally, we noted how our autism can give us an acute perception of detail, and pondered on some of the wonder and beauty that this allows. We critiqued social approbation of a wider focus and suggested that this aspect of autism – as with so many – should be recognised as a difference rather than a deficit.

Issues with the project so far

Although we felt that the Shared Reading of literature was a helpful support to discussion of our autistic experiences, there were issues with the project. The first was that there was a

2. THE SHARED READING PROJECT

limited range of voices being heard. The education level of many of the participants was extremely high; the group included, for example, undergraduates, graduates, doctoral students, MA students, teachers and a solicitor – a wonderful group of people, but hardly typical of the wider population. This, we acknowledged, meant that we were hearing only a limited range of responses, and for the approach to be fully successful a far wider group of participants would need to be heard.

This led us to our second limitation: that the project, by definition, relies on words. However, not all autistic people use words, and those who do not are sorely under-represented in autism research. We know that some people who do not use speech use typing or other forms of augmented communication, and we felt that this could (and we hope will) be used to access the perspectives of this wider group. However, we remained concerned that the use of literature still relied by definition on *words,* and this excludes some people from sharing their experiences.

Although only at a pilot stage we tried to address aspects of this issue through moving from words to 'things' – objects, artefacts, photographs, films, music… anything that could represent autistic experience symbolically.

**

PART TWO:
BEYOND WORDS

We took as our starting point for this pilot using the 'reading' of artefacts the idea of Objects of Reference,[35] sometimes used with people with complex communication needs. In the case of Objects of Reference an object is used to communicate with the person that something is about to happen. In time the person may be able to turn that around and use the object to make a request. In this way a cup may be given to a person to indicate that drinks are about to be served, and the person encouraged to present the cup when they wish to have a drink.

We moved this on to include the concept of metaphor that we had been exploring through the shared reading of the poem to express experiences of autism. We were interested in the potential here for exploration that 'has no right answer', where different and even contradictory understandings can all be valid. We saw Wordsworth's daffodils as representing a crowd of non-autistic people; we also saw their fluttering and dancing as representing autistic flapping and repetitive movements. Both made sense to us, even as they represented opposing ideas. Was there potential, we wondered, to have a similar,

---

[35] Jones, F., Pring, T., & Grove, N. (2002). Developing communication in adults with profound and multiple learning difficulties using objects of reference. International journal of language & communication disorders, 37(2), 173-184.

2. THE SHARED READING PROJECT

open-ended 'shared reading' of an object that represented an aspect of autism for that person ... and what, we considered, would our objects be and why?

Use of symbol for autism has a chequered history. The first — and probably most famous — visual representation of autism is the jigsaw puzzle piece. This was first used by the newly formed National Autistic Society (NAS) in 1963 in a design created by Gerald Gasson which also incorporated the face of a crying child. It has evolved and adapted into many forms, including the autism puzzle piece ribbon used to promote 'Autism Awareness/Acceptance Week'. Importantly, it has been appropriated by the group Autism Speaks, a group seen by many autistic people to be ableist and discriminatory.

Even if we separate the symbol from the groups who use it, the puzzle piece remains problematic as a symbol and is rejected by many within the autism community[36]. The suggestion is that it implies that autism is puzzling, something that is strange to the predominant neurotype population and a mystery that needs 'solving'. It alludes to one of the supposed 'super-skills' of autism, being able to complete complex jigsaw puzzles, sometimes even with the picture turned to the reverse. It usually appears in primary colours, alluding to a children's activity or game, which infantilises autistic people. Perhaps most hurtfully it implies that there is 'something missing' in autistic people,

---

[36] Pellicano, L., Mandy, W., Bölte, S., Stahmer, A., Lounds Taylor, J., & Mandell, D. S. (2018). A new era for autism research, and for our journal. Autism, 22(2), 82-83.

the one puzzle piece being absent rendering the whole puzzle (or person) incomplete.

We discussed the currently more accepted symbol – the neurodiversity rainbow infinity symbol – and what we like and do not like about this. We questioned that, again, in using a rainbow of colours to represent the fullness of diversity, whether this could be taken to be child-like, although we also acknowledged the link to the LGBTQIA+ rainbow and the use of blues and purples to widen inclusivity. We applauded this inclusivity, although some people were concerned that the neurodiversity movement may include so wide a range of presentations that autism itself may feel lost. We discussed the golden infinity symbol as a purely autistic representation and why this might be slower to be adopted.

With all these complexities in mind, we were interested in what symbols the members of the Shared Reading project would bring to represent autism for them. These artefacts and discussion of them were shared in an exhibition at Bishop Grosseteste University in 2022, and some examples are given opposite.

2. THE SHARED READING PROJECT

Before reading further please pause here and take a moment to consider what symbols for autism you would suggest. How and why might this item or artefact represent autism for you?

The items suggested by the group members are given below. Again, just take a moment or two to think about the ways that these might symbolise some aspects of autism, and how you might make meanings that are personal to you.

Artefacts

Rubik's Cube
Timer
Elephant
Twin-lens camera
Wooden toy train
Almost identical t-shirts
Icosahedron (20-sided die)

PARTICIPANTS' ARTEFACTS

Rubik's Cube

At first glance, this symbol may carry much of the stigma of the puzzle piece – it is childish, a toy, something to be 'solved' ... but that was not how it was either presented or received by the group. The contributor, an autistic father of an autistic son, talked about connection, how he and his son found that the cube became a point of contact for them when they could otherwise struggle. The son learned to complete the puzzle through repeating and copying his father's movements, a form of 'shared' activity that the father felt had brought them closer together. They also became interested in 'cube racing' – the completion of different cubes in competition and began watching these events online together with great enjoyment, collecting the statistics and following their chosen champions (many of whom identify as autistic themselves[37]).

In each case the members of the group discussed the object and its potential symbolism away from and beyond that originally intended by the contributor in order to support their own 'reading' of it. Some members were concerned by the suggestion that the cube can be 'solved', but were also interested in the many, many different combinations of colour that can appear on any cube at any time – almost, if not quite, as varied as implied by the infinity symbol[38]. They discussed it as beautiful in its 'unsolved' state, and in its richness of presentation. We discussed the sensory pleasure of turning the layers of the cube through its different axes, and the pleasing 'click' of the layers as they align. We discussed how it is seen as complex, difficult and challenging, and yet is actually very easy to learn. As one member said, "if you make a bit of effort, it is perfectly possible to decode – it just takes a bit of time and attention" … which we felt was an apt comparison with the supposed 'puzzle' of autism.

---

[37] For example, see https://www.npr.org/2023/06/20/1182850678/max-park-speedcube-record-rubiks-cube

[38] 43 quintillion, according to https://artofproblemsolving.com/wiki/index.php/Rubiks_cube

2. THE SHARED READING PROJECT

Timer

The timer – a 'transition support' used frequently with autistic children[39] – breaks time into organised parts. It is used to indicate how long an activity should take, to warn of a change in activity, to limit time spent in a preferred interest. As such, the members of the group felt some hostility to it, although two who are also parents confided that they have and do use a timer with their child, and all agreed to using them routinely in their own lives. This was most commonly through alarms set on their mobile phones or through digital diaries. Many confirmed that the alarms gave security and reduced anxiety, especially around activities such as catching a train or getting off a train at a certain station. One member indicated that the use of a timer in this way helped to "make time manageable" and that it was "essential for organisation, and organisation is certainty: without certainty there is only chaos, which is terrifying".

There was some discussion about the group's initial hostility, and about giving autistic children tools that will be genuinely useful to them in adult life. Although the members who had had timers imposed on them in childhood remembered them with resentment, they still used the strategy voluntarily in maturity. The consensus was that it is different if you choose to set time limits for yourself rather than have them imposed on you. The feeling was that the timer was most frequently used in childhood

---

[39] For example, Hume, K., Sreckovic, M., Snyder, K., & Carnahan, C. R. (2014). Smooth transitions: Helping students with autism spectrum disorder navigate the school day. Teaching Exceptional Children, 47(1), 35-45.

as a tool to limit access to focussed and preferred interests – a way of moving an autistic pupil away from an activity chosen by them and back to one decided by the teacher. To set such a limit oneself (as a reminder) was felt to be wholly healthy, but to have it as a means of compelling a change of activity was felt to be an imposition (even when the rationale for it is understood and accepted).

The group member who donated the timer had been training to be a teacher. He was told to break his lessons into 20-minute sections and took the timer with him into the classroom set at 20-minute intervals. When he was observed and subsequently was 'failed' by his south-of-England university, one of the reasons cited was his rigidity and lack of fluid transition between lesson segments. He presented the timer as his artefact as he felt that it represented his ongoing confusion and sense of hurt that as an autistic person he had followed the instruction "to the letter" and in the way that he had been taught to do, but had still not achieved neurotypical fluency and had not managed to fulfil the requirements of the course.

Elephant

Initially there was puzzlement in the group that an elephant might represent autism. How? Is it because it is large and clumsy? Is it because it could be perceived as threatening?

As members defended the elephant from these accusations, so the animal as a metaphor for autism began to emerge.

2. THE SHARED READING PROJECT

Elephants, we suggested, are highly intelligent and communicate in a sophisticated way with each other, but there are barriers to elephant/people communication[40]. We know through observation and study that they experience emotions that we can recognise, for example that they are capable of grief and mourning, but again this does not manifest itself in the same way as presented by us. An elephant's access to its sensory world is largely through its trunk, which we do not have, and through sounds and seismic communication, that we cannot perceive. There are glimpses of a 'shared world' apparent to us (the example was suggested of elephants 'holding hands' in that a baby elephant will hold onto its mother's tail), but in many ways we live parallel and often (mutually) not fully comprehended existences[41].

We discussed the rumour that elephants are terrified of mice, and the oft-repeated cartoon of the large elephant balancing precariously on a stool while a tiny mouse sits underneath. It was felt that this portrayal, and the mockery implicit in it, captures something of the neurotypical contempt for autistic 'reasonless' fears. A fear is real to the person who feels it, regardless of if that fear is shared with another. We discussed programmes of desensitisation sometimes imposed on autistic children[42] and

---

[40] Langbauer Jr, W. R. (2000). Elephant communication. Zoo Biology: Published in affiliation with the American Zoo and Aquarium Association, 19(5), 425-445.

[41] For more on elephant fact and fiction, see Rothfels, N. (2021). Elephant Trails.

[42] See Lydon, S., Healy, O., O'Callaghan, O., Mulhern, T., & Holloway, J.

the concept that it is apparently socially acceptable to inflict a terrifying situation on an autistic child repeatedly, simply because the terror is not felt by the non-autistic adult.

Twin-lens camera

This was a very specific artefact (it was, in fact, a twin lens Yashica), and its provider was invited to articulate his reasons for presenting it. These were that usually, when taking a picture, it is obvious as the photographer looks at the subject through the lens. However, with this camera, the photographer is looking down and not at the person at all. The interaction is less intense and has an embedded 'courtesy' and respect for private space.

The picture takes longer to create and, once it has been created, cannot easily be changed or edited. The twin lens gives a more accurate image than a digital picture and could therefore be considered to be more honest. It takes time to compose the picture and to take it, and then there is a further wait until the image can be seen. There is a slowness and a time-commitment built into the process. There is no instant gratification.

During the taking of the photo, the photographer is apart and separate but must engage with the subject of the photo – to talk to them to keep them on board, relaxed and still. There is interaction, but this occurs formally and at a distance. There

---

(2015). A systematic review of the treatment of fears and phobias among children with autism spectrum disorders. Review Journal of Autism and Developmental Disorders, 2, 141-154.

2. THE SHARED READING PROJECT

is no eye contact, because the photographer looks down into the lens.

The subject does not appear to be looking directly back either.[43] In this way the camera provides a 'buffer' between people, but the event remains a shared experience. The camera provides a scaffold for the interaction.

This camera has two lenses – the periscope and the one connected to where the film is. One is for perception, and one is for the doing. Like in autism, one is for the taking in from the outside and one is for the presenting back to the outside, and the two are not the same.

The group agreed that in this example digital or mobile phone cameras could be perceived as being like neurotypicals and the twin lens as being like autistic people. The twin lens camera takes more commitment and effort, and the results are not the same as those produced in the more popular way. In some elements they can be seen as lesser – the twin lens is outmoded, lacks flexibility, lacks the built in ability to 'tweak' reality. However, the resulting photographs have their own value in their truth, genuineness and beauty which the more common forms of photography may lack.

---

[43] Eye contact avoidance remains little understood in autism. For a summary of the two main theories, see Stuart, N., Whitehouse, A., Palermo, R., Bothe, E. & Badcock, N. (2023). Eye gaze in autism spectrum disorder: a review of neural evidence for the eye avoidance hypothesis. Journal of Autism and Developmental Disorders, 53(5), 1884-1905.

Wooden toy train

We discussed stereotypes, and how they can also be true. It is a stereotype that autistic people like trains, and that autistic children play with toy railways ... but we also had to admit that there is quite often a truth to it. All of the parents in this group agreed that their autistic children enjoyed playing with train sets to some extent, and some of the autistic adults owned up to reading train timetables for pleasure or to enjoying 'collecting' visits to as many of the UK's stations as possible. We discussed the concepts of predictability, of routine, of scheduling and systemising that trains could bring and how these things can be hugely positive for some autistic people.[44]

We also acknowledged that shared interests are likely to lead to social opportunities for autistic people. I shared information about a colleague whose strong interest was in electricity pylons. He enjoyed visiting them, talking about them, finding out about them and found friendship and belonging in the now sadly extinct *Pylon Appreciation Society*. We rejected the shorthand title for autistic people of 'trainspotters' but have enough self-awareness to acknowledge that it may well be that, whilst not all autistic people are trainspotters, certainly many trainspotters are autistic!

The particular train being offered as an artefact was 'well loved', indeed appeared rather battered. The contributor shared that

---

[44] See, for example, Overskeid, G. (2016). Systemizing in autism: The case for an emotional mechanism. New Ideas in Psychology, 41, 18-22.

2. THE SHARED READING PROJECT

her son was carrying the particular toy shortly after he was diagnosed as autistic. He dropped it as they were crossing a busy road and slipped her hand to run back, only being stopped at the last moment by his mother catching onto the hood of his jacket. The train was run over by a speeding car – hence its battered appearance – but her son was not. As she said, her son being hit by a car would have been a tragedy; finding out that he is autistic was not. The train put things in perspective for her at the time, and she values it still.

Almost identical t-shirts

The three child-sized t-shirts under discussion all featured the cover of the Beatles' *Abbey Road* album. This led to some confusion amongst the group members who were distracted by the image and missed the point of the t-shirts, which included that they were good quality, soft, old, much washed and had a printed rather than sewn-in label. The autistic child of the group member had been given one of the t-shirts some years before and he wanted to wear it all the time. He wore it daily, under his school uniform, to bed … and was distressed when it had to be taken away to be washed. As well as developing "the fastest overnight wash and dry turnaround in the land", the parents went onto second-hand sites and found a near-identical shirt. The child accepted the substitute, and all seemed fine, except of course that the child was growing so this had to be repeated many times. The group member shared that she and her husband, friends and relatives were all adept and keeping their eyes open in charity shops throughout the country for these particular t-shirts.

We discussed the lengths that we will go to – for ourselves and for our children – to find items of clothing that 'work' for us. One member described his discomfort with new clothes, and how he too chooses to shop second hand, not merely for financial or ethical reasons but because the clothes are usually soft and well washed. We agreed that clothing conventions and uniforms in both school and the workplace can exclude many autistic people who find what they are required to wear uncomfortable to the point of positive discomfort. Some members focussed on the smell of clothes, and how certain fabric cleaners or softeners leave a repellent residue. The general consensus was that clothes that smelt of the wearer were often rather pleasant, and the need to wash clothes and to wear clean clothes was for some very much a social convention rather than instinctive.

The t-shirts being the same prompted a discussion of the work of Andy Warhol and his printing of repeated images, either all the same as with his print of Campbell's soup cans or with colour differences as in his work on Marilyn Munroe. We acknowledged that consensus of opinion is that Warhol would, now, be recognised as autistic[45] and we discussed the impact of famous people who are 'diagnosed' posthumously.

---

[45] See, for example, section on Warhol's work in Roth, I. (2020). Autism, creativity and aesthetics. Qualitative Research in Psychology, 17(4), 498-508.

We concluded by returning to the 'red herring' of the t-shirts being about the Beatles. We thought that this was an excellent analogy for autistic focus as the child has no interest in the music of the group at all and equates the famous picture of the four crossing the zebra crossing purely with comfort. As so often happens in autism, the focus was not quite what would be expected by the 'outside world'.

Icosahedron

An icosahedron (20-sided die) was suggested as a symbol for autism because with it the player can "manage a whole created world" through gaming. It symbolised the detail and complexity of a world built in imagination, separate from the real world in which the autistic gamer lives. We discussed escapism and whether withdrawal into fictional worlds is healthy, conceding that to do so in fiction (as in the worlds of JRR Tolkien or even JK Rowling) is more 'acceptable' socially than to move into that of gaming. We felt that this reflects a certain academic snobbery. Several of the group members enjoyed Role-Playing Games (RPGs), and Dungeons and Dragons in particular.[46] As with the interest in trains we were keen to identify the strong and positive social contact elements of being involved in an interest of this kind.[47]

---

[46] See, for example, Valorozo-Jones, C. (2021). Neurodiversity, Dungeons, and Dragons: A guide to transforming and enriching TTRPGs for Neurodivergent Adults OR The Neurodivergent Player's Handbook;

[47] See, for example, Fein, E. (2015). Making meaningful worlds: Role-playing subcultures and the autism spectrum. Culture, Medicine, and Psychiatry, 39, 299-321.

We were drawn to the fact that the die is 20 sided, being so much more complex than the traditional 6-sided version. We felt that there were connections here with the many manifestations and experiences of autism, how it is multifaceted. We also accepted that, in gaming, the 20-sided die is the 'most important' as it decides so many elements of play. It is random ... but brings order to that randomness in that one of the possibilities must be the outcome.

We agreed that the shape is pleasingly tactile and that the multiple faces of the die used in gaming are interesting in their own right.[48] Polyhedral dice have survived from Ancient Greek and Roman times, with the icosahedron being the most frequent.[49] We also agreed that tactile and auditory benefits of rolling a physical die make this infinitely preferable to using an on-line virtual alternative. We liked that the die is an accepted recognisable symbol for the gaming world and felt that it worked as a symbol for at least some aspects of autism.

Summary of responses to the artefacts

There were a wide range of issues discussed in relation to using these various items as symbols for autism, and the approach appears to have some potential.

---

[48] Borodina, K., Aslam, H., & Brown, J. A. (2019, August). You have my sword; and my bow; and my axe: player perceptions of odd shaped dice for dungeons & dragons. In Proceedings of the 14th International Conference on the Foundations of Digital Games (pp. 1-6).

[49] https://www.metmuseum.org/art/collection/search/551072

2. THE SHARED READING PROJECT

- We discussed the beauty of diversity, and how recognising that having a wider range of differences in the ways that autism presents and is experienced can add to its richness. We asserted that autism can be better understood if people are willing to try, and that simply stating that it is a 'puzzle' is both patronising and lazy.
- We considered the differences in sensory experience and in communication between neurodivergent and neurotypical people, and how just because one individual does not receive something as communication, it does not mean that nothing is being imparted.
- We discussed patience and how it may be that an autistic way of working may be slower or take more time, but that it may also have an honesty and integrity that quicker approaches may not.
- We thought about stereotypes and how they can sometimes carry elements of truth, and how sharing of autistic interests can sometimes lead to hugely rich social networks. We talked about the joy of shared world-building where the context of that world is clear and inclusive.
- We talked about meeting autistic needs, about how supports put into place in childhood can or could be carried forward by that child as useful into adulthood.
- Finally, we considered acceptance of autism – of parents of their children, of each other and of ourselves.

Issues with the approach

Although we enjoyed moving beyond literature to the exploration of artefacts as symbols for autism, there remains the issue that these discussions still used spoken words. The artefacts do not carry intrinsic meaning – or rather, they carry many meanings, and it is only through discussion that some of these as they pertain to autism may be teased out. We are hoping to expand our approach to include autistic people who do not use spoken language, including those who use Augmentative and Alternative Communication (AAC), but are still some distance from exploring this successfully. We plan to continue this research moving forward.

However, one aspect of AAC is typing – and this can be very powerful way for autistic people to be heard[50]. During the Covid-19 'lockdowns' when many lessons went online, teachers were astonished by the typed contributions of many of their pupils[51]. As part of the Shared Reading project, we had two typed contributions sent in to the group by autistic contributors (not, in fact, by people who do not use spoken language, but simply as a preferred form on this occasion) and I believe they add considerable richness. They are included overleaf in their entireties.

---

[50] Sequenzia, A. & Grace, E. (Eds) (2015). Typed Words, Loud Voices. Autonomous Press. USA

[51] See Roitsch, J., Moore, R. L., & Horn, A. L. (2021). Lessons learned: What the COVID-19 global pandemic has taught us about teaching, technology, and students with autism spectrum disorder. Journal of Enabling Technologies, 15(2), 108-116.

2. THE SHARED READING PROJECT

Typed contributions

1. Smooth vs spiky balls

Both smooth and spiky balls are capable of rolling along. Occasionally the spiky one might prang you - not intentionally, maybe pick it up more carefully next time?

There are many more smooth balls so seeing a spiky one can be surprising.

There are spiky balls that have been smoothed - so if they didn't want you to know, you wouldn't. Some of them were smoothed so long ago and so subtly that they didn't realise it either. Unfortunately, the smoothing process can take an awful lot of effort, energy, experience, time, and is sometimes – parts of them are being removed after all – harmful.

They also end up not quite smooth, or smaller than they were.

Smooth balls appear to roll and roll effortlessly (unless they hit a major obstacle). Sometimes the spiky balls bounce around major obstacles (spikes make for less predictable bounces) but get stuck on a seemingly flat surface.

Sometimes the spikes hold onto things, it can take more effort to remove things from their surface (and they don't really understand why you want to do that anyway).

Contributor's note: Autism is greatly varied, I know that there are differences across the spectrum, as well as across sex, class, culture, and so on. I have tried to paint both balls as 'neutral' - I dislike the habit of pitting 'neurodivergent' and 'neurotypical' people against each other. Can't we all just get along?

2. Pasta

My object to describe autism would be a piece of shell pasta (or conchiglie, if you're posher than me. Or Italian).

This could well be because, just as all shapes of pasta are different and are more or less beneficial in certain situations, so too are different facets of autism or, in fact, different autistic people. Autism is as varied as the world of pasta shapes.

However, I shan't be doing that.

I think my most prevalent autistic trait, especially in childhood, was my attitude towards food.

2. THE SHARED READING PROJECT

I went through a phase where I would only eat yellow food – yellow being my favourite colour – which was only broken when I discovered that I could mask the flavours of most foods I didn't like with tomato ketchup. I've now graduated from ketchup to using spice to hide the foods I don't like and, although I am more adventurous than I once was with food, I would still be classed as a 'picky eater'.

Although I didn't have the capacity to explain it at the time, my restricted diet was to do with sensory issues and, I think, experiencing flavours and textures in more vivid or different ways to my neurotypical peers. (The number of times I have been told that cucumber "doesn't have a flavour" is astronomical. It most definitely does, and that flavour is gross.).

I was very lucky, however, that my parents never saw my picky eating as a behaviour issue, something to be stamped out, and were happy to let me continue with my strange diet of yellow foods – lots of scrambled eggs and pasta with cheese – and then only a few meals which I would eat in tight rotation.

I have also chosen this pasta shape because it is my favourite. I love all pasta and I am aware that the shapes are designed to hold different types of sauce etc., but some of the shapes are simply more pleasing to me than others. Twisty pasta (that's fusilli) ranks last, followed by tubes (penne), followed by bows (farfalle), and then, crowning them all, the shell. It has the most pleasing feeling in my mouth, the ability to hold almost a small spoonful of sauce, and the delightful challenge of it sometimes springing off your fork if you stabbed it the wrong way. It is, hands down, the king of pasta shapes for me.

As well as not forcing me to eat the foods I strongly did not want to, my parents also actively interacted with my strangenesses – apparently having strong views on pasta shapes is strange to some – with regards to food and nurtured my strong-mindedness. I was allowed, each week on the weekly shop, to decide which shape of pasta we were to have. The answer was usually shell, although I did sometimes branch out for a bow if I wanted some fun.

It would have been very easy for my parents to say that the shape of pasta I ate didn't matter, and that, actually, Spaghetti Bolognese requires spaghetti and so that is what we shall eat. They were, after all, the adults, and I was the child.

Instead, we had many meals of shell Bolognese – Conchiglie Bolognese, perhaps – and I remember them with great happiness.

**

2. THE SHARED READING PROJECT

Each of these contributions adds to the richness of perceptions of autism shared in this book, and each employs a lovely light-touch sense of humour. The extended metaphor of spiky vs smooth balls positions autism firmly as a difference not a deficit, and this enables the writer to challenge the odd notion of hiding difference, identifying the damage that autistic camouflaging may produce when we 'end up not quite smooth, or smaller than [we] were'. Why, the writer asks, can't we all just get along?

The second piece plays skilfully and deftly with the notion of 'special interests', as autistic enthusiasms are so readily labelled by parts of the neurotypical community. The writer raises their metaphorical eyebrow at the idea that having favourite shapes of pasta may be strange (having already contextualised the piece with a sly nod towards this notion of being Italian!), and the piece is a warm tribute to a childhood spent with a feelings of acceptance and belonging.

These considerations of typed contributions, and the process of creating meaning-making through the written word, brings us nicely to the next chapter of this book. In this Olivia will discuss their creative writing project undertaken with a group of autistic students and how this explores how the process of meaning-making through the written word can be a hugely useful tool, allowing us to explore our lives and experiences in metaphorical and understandable ways.

**

CHAPTER 3

Creative writing project

Olivia Macnab

Meaning-Making through Creative Writing

In the previous chapter we discussed how we could apply the written word to our own experiences, taking serious literature and interpreting its relevance to our lives. In this chapter, I will discuss a project which aims to perform the opposite approach: to take our lives and experiences and apply them to the written word.

Using examples from both serious literature and my own writing, I guided my participants through a process to develop their creative writing skills, through which they produced a number of pieces of creative writing expressing aspects of their experience. Some of these pieces were then developed into a theatrical performance, in which many of the participants took part performing each other's written work.

The project was guided by the principles of Applied Drama, in accordance with my area of study. In order to provide context, we shall start with a short introduction to this field.

An Introduction to Applied Drama and Community Projects

Applied Drama has many definitions, as umbrella terms often do, but broadly it refers to the practice of collaborative and participatory drama created in order to help people. The form grew originally from Dorothy Heathecote's educational drama practice, now generally referred to as Process Drama[52], the Prison Theatre movements of the 1970s[53], and Augusto Boal's Theatre for the Oppressed[54]. Today, the term is often overused, but may apply to the practice of Theatre in Education, Process Drama, Theatre for Development, Prison Theatre, Hospital Theatre, Dramatherapy, and other uses of dramatic and theatrical techniques. Specifically it refers to work undertaken with often marginalised communities of people, with the intentions of empowerment, enabling, and providing artistic experiences to those who are often left out of them.

---

[52] Davis, D., Bolton, G. M., & Fleming, M. (Michael P.). (2014). Imagining the real: Towards a new theory of drama in education (1–1 online resource (xv, 179 pages)). Institute of Education Press. htps://search.ebscohost.com/login.aspx?direct=true&scope=site&db=nlebk&db=nlabk&AN=1642887

[53] Thompson, J. (1998). Prison Theatre: Perspectives & Practices. Jessica Kingsley Publishers Ltd.

[54] Boal, A. (2002). Games for actors and non-actors (2nd ed, 1–1 online resource (xxix, 301 pages): illustrations). Routledge. http://www.dawsonera.com/abstract/9780203994818

3. CREATIVE WRITING PROJECT

Applied Drama is often considered to have eight principles, compiled by Philip Taylor in 2003[55], stating that the work must:

- Be well-researched
- Offer significant opportunity for participants to interpret and direct it
- Demonstrate a variety of options for interpretation of aims
- Offer participants tasks in which they are empowered and practise as the protagonist
- Tackle conflict, dialogue and dilemma in its prompts and themes
- Interrogate the current and future opportunities for participants and their interaction with the communities around them
- Provide an aesthetic medium in which to tackle these issues
- Empower participants to use their voices

During my research on the subject, I had the opportunity to develop my own Community Project. Throughout this I was required to select or form my community group, based on my preferred practices, prior research and interests, before researching and identifying what might be useful for that group or community, and how best to target those aims. I then developed a well planned and useful project, featuring a

---

[55] Taylor, P. (2003). Applied theatre: Creating transformative encounters in the community. Heinemann.

final showing and/or legacy, and lead, directed and facilitated sessions throughout the project. Finally, I evaluated and assessed the project after its completion.

Initial Research and Development

Throughout the initial research and development of the project, I began by identifying the areas I wanted to work in. I was diagnosed as autistic in my second year of university, at nineteen years old, though I began researching the identity and considering its relevance to my life well before that time. As I have examined my own life and development, it has always been clear to me how essential drama and creative writing have been for me, and so ever since beginning to study Applied Drama I have been excited by its applications with neurodivergent people. Therefore, I intended to develop a project which focussed on neurodiversity and the autism community.

I began by researching communities and community practice, and quickly grew concerned by the often divisional nature of the concept[56]. In research, communities largely fall into four categories. These include communities of location, which are based on physical areas, communities of interest, which are based on hobbies and ideas, communities of practice, who engage in activities together, and communities of identity, which are based on identities and labels. Very often, communities can

---

[56] Nicholson, H. (2014). Applied drama: The gift of theatre (Second edition). Palgrave Macmillan.

fall under multiple of these categories, and the lines between them are heavily blurred. And while they can give us useful shorthands and provide identity, security and friendship, they are also increasingly romanticised, and can encourage an 'us' and 'them' mentality. In addition, communities of identity can also lead to everyone within the community being painted with the same brush and viewed with an often stereotypical lens, or 'homogenised'.

While examining this more negative impact that communities can bring, I was struck by the similarities between it and the othering and homogenisation so often experienced by, for want of a better shorthand, the neurodivergent community. So often, neurodivergent people are set apart from their peers simply by virtue of thinking and interacting differently, and face significant challenges of stigma, stereotypes and infantilisation. This remains present even in the research community. So many projects with neurodivergent people are led by neurotypical researchers and, whatever intentions they begin with, fall into the trap of condescending to their participants, denying their autonomy and taking evidence from their parents or carers rather than from neurodivergent people themselves[57]. In addition, neurodivergent people often experience a homogenisation of care. Autism alone is widely understood to be a spectrum, and it is undeniable that no two autistic people are exactly alike or experience the exact same sensory environments, social

---

[57] Massa, A., DeNigris, D., & Gillespie-Lynch, K. (2020). Theatre as a tool to reduce autism stigma? Evaluating 'Beyond Spectrums'. Research in Drama Education: The Journal of Applied Theatre and Performance, 25(4), 613–630.

differences or triggers. When neurodivergency as an umbrella term is brought into the equation, this becomes even more the case. And yet, so often, neurodivergent people get the same broad-strokes, non-specific care and provision[58]. This is especially the case at university, and though steps are being and have been made to enable a more accessible system and tailored support package, the sector as a whole often expects neurodivergent people to require the same technology and support systems as each other. Finally, neurodivergent and neurotypical people often struggle to understand each other due to what is known as the double empathy barrier[59] – the fact neurodivergent people and neurotypical people's brains work differently presents difficulties in both sides empathising with the other, though the blame for this is so often placed solely upon neurodivergent people.

Taking these factors into account, I devised a project which intended to bring two communities together from the start, working with two community groups to encourage empathy and understanding across a broad spectrum of identities and experiences, before bringing these increases in understanding to a wider audience. As well as tackling these empathetic challenges and divisions between communities, I also intended to target a number of other issues faced by the neurodivergent community, especially those who are students.

---

[58] Berney, T. (2021). Autistic doctors: Is there a problem? Good Autism Practice (GAP), 22(2), 40–43.

[59] Milton, D. E. (2012). On the ontological status of autism: The 'double empathy problem'. Disability & society, 27(6), 883-887

Firstly, and most importantly for me, a stereotype remains even in the academic world which claims that neurodivergent people are not creative and understand only that which is logical and literal. A lack of understanding of metaphor, for example, still remains on the diagnostic criteria for autism[60], despite studies disproving this fact and evidencing that, in some cases, neurodivergent people develop more novel, creative metaphors than their neurotypical counterparts[61]. As a writer, dramatist, storyteller and artist, creative expression has been utterly integral to every part of my life, and I quite often interpret my experiences and understandings of the world around me through creative mediums. And yet as an autistic person, the world around me claims that this is impossible or abnormal. I therefore intend to challenge this stereotype and evidence how creative autistic people can be.

Additionally, neurodivergent people may struggle with the concept of identity, undergoing a process known as 'masking' or 'camouflaging'[62], during which they deliberately disguise their neurodivergent traits and act neurotypical, often in a way that

---

[60] American Psychiatric Association. (2013). Diagnostic and statistical manual of mental disorders (5th ed.) Washington, DC.

[61] For example, Kasirer, A., & Mashal, N. (2014). Verbal creativity in autism: Comprehension and generation of metaphoric language in high-functioning autism spectrum disorder and typical development. Frontiers in Human Neuroscience, 8. https://doi.org/10.3389/fnhum.2014.00615

[62] Cook, J., Hull, L., Crane, L., & Mandy, W. (2021). Camouflaging in autism: A systematic review [Preprint]. Open Science Framework. https://doi.org/10.31219/osf.io/u5b9e

reflects those around them, in order to protect themselves. This process is exhausting, requiring neurodivergent people to suppress instinctive behaviours and at the same time force themselves to adopt unnatural ones. However, it often (especially in those who were diagnosed after early childhood years) happens without the person fully being aware of it and can lead to uncertainty over what is truly part of oneself and what is borrowed from others or forced on by the mask.

Finally, the neurodivergent community faces an extreme prevalence of mental health issues[63]. Neurodivergent people are far more likely to experience depression and anxiety, and in a world which is not designed for them and does not understand them, support is hard to access and far too often unhelpful for the specific needs of the neurodivergent experience. It is important for projects developed with neurodivergent people in mind to assist them in developing healthy coping mechanisms, and the protection of fiction can be extremely helpful in this[64]. In addition, drama and creative writing can both aid in social, emotional, verbal and written literacy[65], presenting

---

[63] Gegelashvili, M. (2022). Autism and Depression. Georgian Medical News, 7–8, 54–57. And Gillott, A., Furniss, F., & Walter, A. (2001). Anxiety in High-Functioning Children with Autism. Autism, 5(3), 277–286. https://doi.org/10.1177/1362361301005003005

[64] Davis, D., Bolton, G. M., & Fleming, M. (Michael P.). (2014). Imagining the real: Towards a new theory of drama in education (1–1 online resource (xv, 179 pages)). Institute of Education Press. https://search.ebscohost.com/login.aspx?direct=true&scope=site&db=nlebk&db=nlabk&AN=1642887

[65] Deveney, C., & Lawson, P. (2022). Writing your way to well-being: An IPA analysis of the therapeutic effects of creative writing on mental health

opportunities for neurodivergent people to grow their skills in a far more nurturing and autonomous way than most research and upskilling projects allow.

Through this research, the basic intention of Identity Inclusion was formed: to develop a project with two communities on campus. At least one of these was explicitly centred on neurodivergence, with the project presenting opportunity for creative expression, exploration of identity, increasing soft skills, and overcoming empathy barriers, and which would have both an immediate and legacy impact for a wider audience.

A summary of research

Thus far, we have discussed the research process leading up to the development of this project. This is what was found:

- Applied Drama has many definitions, but its principles, designed to encourage the use of theatrical techniques to empower and enfranchise specific, often marginalised communities, has exciting potential for applications with neurodivergent people.
- Communities can be divisional and oppressive, and while encouraging community development can be important, it is also important to encourage more intersectional communities and overcome barriers between communities.

---

and the processing of emotional difficulties. Counselling and Psychotherapy Research, 22(2), 292–300. https://doi.org/10.1002/capr.12435

- Autism and neurodivergency are often homogenised and stereotyped, and there remains a variety of barriers to autistic expression, and to neurotypical people's empathy with and understanding of the autistic experience.
- Some of the important issues to tackle include the stereotype that autistic people are solely literal and logical, autistic people's struggles with introspection, masking and identity, and the prevalence of mental health issues in neurodivergent people.

Identity Inclusion: The Process

Having completed this research and development process, I then developed the project that would become *Identity Inclusion*. Over the course of twelve weeks, I guided a group of participants drawn from both the Students' Union Creative Writing Society and the university's Autism Resources and Community Hub along a process of creative writing, editing and performance. From this project, my participants and I developed a number of pieces of poetry, prose and script, before selecting excerpts of them to develop into a performance of dramatic readings given to a wider audience.

For the interested reader, curious about exactly how the process worked, or those who might wish to develop their own projects, I will now detail the three stages of the process: Writing, Editing and Performance.

3. CREATIVE WRITING PROJECT

Over the course of the Writing phase, I provided my participants with an introduction to three formats of creative writing: poetry, prose and script. Each workshop began with an entry activity, usually a short-form, light-touch prompt, just to get our creative muscles flowing. These included a haiku, a piece of dialogue in which each new line had to start with the next letter of the alphabet, or a short description using the five senses, for example. After our creative brains were engaged, I brought a teaching point forward for discussion, using examples to illustrate the idea I was planning to explore, and encouraging an open discussion about how that idea was developed and where and why it was useful. Being an introduction to these three forms of writing, these teaching points involved development of 'jumping-off' skills such as the format of script writing, the concept of narrative voice, or an understanding of rhythm and rhyme. After my participants had gleaned an understanding, we then spent roughly twenty minutes free writing, based on the prompt I brought to the group (you can see the majority of the prompts I offered in the anthology below), and trying to bring out that teaching point through our writing. Finally, another short-form closure activity was used to shake off the space and move back into the 'real world'.

The second stage of the process was Editing. The bane of many writers, I aimed to craft a way to make the editorial process enjoyable for myself just as much as for my participants. The workshops followed a similar format to that of the Writing stage, with a handful of key differences. Entry and closure activities began to introduce more improvisational and performance-based techniques in order to begin to grow my participants' confidence in performance, and teaching points introduced more challenging concepts such as literary techniques, complex character motivations, and integrated plot. Writing time now contained two prompts, one being a prompt used during the Writing phase, and the other being an Editing prompt aiming to encourage the development of that piece of writing further. I encouraged my participants (and always tried myself) to use these sessions to edit our previous pieces, but this was not essential and sometimes people preferred to write something new.

The final phase of the project concerned Performance, which was the part people often said they felt most daunted by and least likely to participate in at the beginning of the project. I extended the session lengths for this in order to ensure we had enough time for performance development, and while sessions still began and ended with an entry and closure activity, these were now largely focussed on preparing our voices, bodies and minds for performance. It was important to strike a balance between accessing the protection of fiction (granted when performing a fictional scenario, allowing one to distance oneself from the situation being performed and protect one's emotions)[66] and enjoying the empowerment that comes from one's voice being seen, heard and projected. Therefore, my participants and I

---

[66] Davis, D., Bolton, G. M., & Fleming, M. (Michael P.). (2014). Imagining the real: Towards a new theory of drama in education (1–1 online resource (xv, 179 pages)). Institute of Education Press. https://search.ebscohost.com/login.aspx?direct=true&scope=site&db=nlebk&db=nlabk&AN=1642887

3. CREATIVE WRITING PROJECT

each directed our own pieces and performed in each other's. This meant that we were able to empower and promote our voices without making ourselves too vulnerable, and also grew my participants' directing abilities as well as performance skills.

In order to showcase the wonderful writing that emerged, we held a miniature festival, featuring a book fair with local authors, the performance itself, and a pub quiz at the Students' Union bar that evening. The performance itself contrasted the pieces of writing with excerpts from the DSM-5 and other quotes about autism, and had a finale featuring an international group of neurodivergent volunteers who wrote, drew or spoke the words 'we are human' alongside my actors, before the audience were encouraged to join in. This was all curated to encourage a wider audience, and with it a greater empathic impact and more intersectional community building.

All of my group members asked to be a part of the performance, and one participant who had seemed the most daunted by the prospect even requested to have more spoken lines during the piece. One of my favourite memories of the entire project was leaving the stage after performing one of my participants' words to find them awaiting me, punching the air and silently screaming in delight. All my participants were empowered by the project, and further, got great joy from the sensation of performance.

Perhaps, though, the best way to evidence the impact of an artistic project is simply to show you it. So without further ado, I pass over to the words of my participants themselves.

IDENTITY INCLUSION: AN ANTHOLOGY

[Please note: some of the writing in this section contains mature language. There are also some grammatical errors or words that may not make total sense, which are identified with 'sic'. These have all been left unedited in the final pieces, in order to preserve the natural creative voice of my participants.]

CONTENTS

Poetry
An Organised Life
Sensory Experiences
Unprompted

Prose
Alphabet Conversation
Your Favourite Place on Campus
A Conversation with your Younger Self

Script
A Conversation with your Younger Self (Cont.)
A Conversation Between a Modern-Day Antagonist and

Protagonist
The Opening Scene of a Movie About your Life

3. CREATIVE WRITING PROJECT

POETRY

An Organised Life

Much poetry takes a very structured form, with set rhythm and rhyme schemes and a pace or a beat to them. For an autistic person, structure and routine can be very important, though many of us still feel that despite our appreciation of structure, our lives don't feel very together!

Think about what an 'Organised Life' means to you, and whether you feel that your current life is particularly organised. How could you express that in poetic form? Spend some time thinking and see if you can write a few verses of poetry based on this prompt.

Participant Responses

As you read, take some time to absorb the words on the page, and compare them to your own work, or to each other. Think about the diversity of experiences and meanings expressed throughout the pieces.

An Organised Life (Or Not for Me)

I dislike Chaos.
The House is Very messy.
Someone starts shouting.
I don't notice messy rooms.
Mess is mine, someone presumes.
My perception is (one syllable) poor.
often walk into doors.
I watch the autumn leaves, fall
Outside, i am not allowed.
Days on windowsills.

3. CREATIVE WRITING PROJECT

Burnout

Hitting limits
"You do too much"
Functional
At least, as such.
Forgetting things
The past few days
Was coping, now
My brain is haze
Nothing left
My energy
Sapping strength
Routine can't keep
My brain in line
But still I move
Keep pressing on
I cannot lose
Thanking diary
My second brain
Keeping track
Of every day
Lessons learnt
And yet, and still
To find a balance

Takes some skill
I try, I try
Myself to shape
Morning, evening
Routines I make
They help, they do
These things curated
Cueing sleep and
Wake, unhated
And yet, I know
They take up time
My spoons march off
To war in line
"You do too much"
I know, I know
But things to drop
My sanity own
I try, I have
Techniques in place
To give me rest
To give me grace
Organised
They see in me
Reliable
Is that all they see?

3. CREATIVE WRITING PROJECT

Listen, listen

I fall apart

I break my bones

I break my heart

Functional

I look, I mask

Powerful

But it can't last

Imposter Syndrome

Rears its head

You're faking it

My heart is lead

My name is not

Reliable

I want to scream

I'm disabled

I cannot be

Your inspiration

Standards held

Above my station

"You do too much"

Please look, please see

Too much is

Expected of me

CREATIVITY IN AUTISM

Busy Lives and Shining Moons

How can I find the time to only find my life's a mess
And if I clean it up there's less
I just want to give you my love
But more I do, there's just more of
Work and rest and pitiless strife
To always keep you from my life
Well, succeeded I, writing a poem
So maybe I should not moan
Goodnight, my sweet, I'll see you soon
Beneath a gorgeous shining moon

**

Discussion

Within these pieces, you can find three very different interpretations of the prompt, and three interesting and well-worked meanings developed from the same prompt, featuring highly creative metaphor and imagery.

The author of the first piece was often told that they have limited perception and decided that their life was not particularly organised upon seeing the prompt, so they wrote about their experiences of home and inability to spot mess. They wrote about autumn leaves because they are often like this – "it seems great from the outside but can be quite soggy and messy on the ground, and people don't often notice that they are so distracted about how it looks like on the trees".

When we discussed the poem they indicated that they particularly like the last line because it brings out the duality of emotion that can be expressed through writing. They are able to enjoy the leaves on the trees and express their delight in that, but it also brings a tinge of sadness – they could be outside, but their chores aren't done and their life isn't organised enough.

Similarly, the author of the second piece felt that organisation was a complicated subject for them at the time. This piece was written in the middle of a major episode of burnout, inspired by that experience, and the complex feelings this person had about the compliment 'reliable'. As they articulated, "So often, those of us who consistently do well, are consistently present and helpful, become taken for granted, and anything perceived as less than 100% by others causes shock and anger. When you're disabled or neurodivergent, and physically can't give 100% all the time, that becomes even more complicated."

Considering an inability to give 100% also fed into the third author's writing. This poem was inspired by the author's new (at time of writing) relationship, and the busy lives they and their partner were living at the time. They were trying to get ready for the next stage of their lives, while simultaneously dealing with a number of difficult, challenging circumstances. As they described to me, it was somewhat of a baptism of fire; "I wrote the poem because I felt like I didn't have as much time for my partner."

This person has enjoyed creating things and exploring words for a long time and enjoys playing role-playing games and engaging with fantasy worlds. They enjoyed the opportunity given by this project to explore more of themselves through fiction and have since taken up writing on a more serious and focussed level than ever before.

Sensory Experiences

For many autistic people, sensory experiences are a defining part of existence. These can be positive or negative – perhaps the most common experience many people will think of will be sensory overload. This occurs when sensory stimuli such as bright lights or types of noise become too much, which can sometimes cause an autistic person to enter shutdown or meltdown[67]*. However, for many autistic people, as well as certain things being negative experiences, there are other things which can be hugely enriching. Certain colours, textures, tastes and so forth can be considered safe and, in many cases, be something that an autistic person will actively seek. This was something I wanted to encourage my participants to explore in depth, enabling them to write about how they experienced the stimuli in the world around them.*

Consider your own experience of the world. Are there certain things that are safe or desirable sensory experiences to you?

---

[67] Weber, C., Krieger, B., Häne, E., Yarker, J., & McDowall, A. (n.d.). Physical workplace adjustments to support neurodivergent workers: A systematic review. Applied Psychology, n/a(n/a). https://doi.org/10.1111/apps.12431

3. CREATIVE WRITING PROJECT

Are there certain things that awaken different memories? Are there stimuli that are bad for you or cause you to feel overwhelmed? What do you want to express about how you see, hear, smell, touch and taste the world? See if you can write a few verses of poetry about these ideas.

Participant Responses

As you read, take some time to absorb the words on the page, and compare them to your own work, or to each other. Think about the diversity of experiences and meanings expressed throughout the pieces.

Sensory Overload

what is it like to not have the ringing
the squealing in your ears
the clench of your jaw when someone eats
the vomit from a fork
it's the needles in my sinuses
and how sometimes i enjoy them
it's the hands i hate unless they're yours
tightness in my eyes and nausea bleeding to my skull
it's the fluorescents
the lights are the prickling on my stomach
no, my shoulders, no, my hands, no, my neck, no, my ankles
and it burns and it reminds me of
people i'm not allowed to remember
stop texting me you know i hate it
who invited you
i feel like my mind is
constantly screaming
come here and get away from me.

3. CREATIVE WRITING PROJECT

Yellow

Sunshine, daisies, butter mellow

I think my favourite colour is yellow

It sends such joy into my life

My gender and my colour wife

My favourite colour once was red

I painted where I rest my head

The colour of hearts, held

in pounding beat

it throbs

that means it's my favourite

right?
and yet

and yet

does it hurt or help?

Nowadays I know myself

I know my mental space and health

I mark in every space I meet

The colours each one I must greet

In golden light I find myself

bright
too much

is still not me

but if the light has golden shine
I usually feel dandy and fine
but white
is bright
no matter what
and blue, when used
to light a room
can spiral
like a helterskelter in the park
I used to love
That was yellow, too.
When flashes

flare
into my brain

the rhythm breaks
But so many things
Feel helpful to me through the years
music lilting in my ears
While gentle colour changing light
Protects me when nonverbal mind
Reflects exhaustion from my days
Spent toiling in the sunlit haze
So often hid with my sunshades
Despite my love of golden light

3. CREATIVE WRITING PROJECT

> And sunshine, daisies, butter mellow
> Make joy within me as I grow
> As those experiences I seek
> Grant freedom from the ones which reek
> And so I still maintain my love
> For yellow, my peace offering, my dove.

Discussion

The author of the first piece examined the negative sensory experiences that can come from autism, exploring the sensation of sensory overload. They describe it as causing a "visceral, physical reaction...sort of like cutlery on plates". The word choice and structure of this poem aims to capture that feeling, expressing the experience of sensory overload using language.

This person enjoys writing and playing with words because it is an important part of who they are. They also say that they love words because their "limit is the language itself", and that "there are always going to be things I can't express, that I can't put down because that is a limitation of the English language, and I think that's so fascinating...there are things that we don't have words for, and I think that's so cool, and that's why I like writing, because I like finding new ways to explore and express things that maybe you can't."

In contrast, the author of the second piece aimed to capture a more positive experience, namely their love for the colour yellow, and how this can be associated with their growing understanding of themselves and their needs. They were inspired by their childhood spent undiagnosed, saying that "I used to think red was my favourite colour because it throbbed every time I looked at it, which made it different than all the others. I thought that's what everyone was sort of talking about."

Their writing is often heavily inspired by the small beauties they see in the world around them and the little joys you can get from all sorts of things. In a similar manner to how yellow brightens up a space or an outfit, they hope to shine a little sunshine into your life with their work.

Unprompted

In conjunction with the explorations of identity and empowerment of autistic voice, Identity Inclusion aimed to encourage its participants to engage in writing for enjoyment and expression outside of the sessions. One participant requested that such an unprompted piece be entered into the anthology, particularly due to its explorations of identity discovery.

Through this poem, the author attempts to explore the age-old question: Who am I? Take some time before you read this poem to consider what answers you might come to in relation to such a question. Do they include labels? How could you express your feelings about your identity through poetry?

3. CREATIVE WRITING PROJECT

As you read, take some time to absorb the words on the page, and compare them to your own work.

Who Am I?

The questions that people ask me are:
Who are you?
Are you rich or poor?
Are you lonely or in a crew?
What is your sexuality?
What are your dreams?
How will you achieve them?
What are your schemes?
The questions come and go
But the first one stick in my head
Who I am?
When I leave my bed?
I am me and that is the end.

This person has been inspired in their writing in recent years by the journeys of self-discovery and understandings of labels that they have seen around them since starting university. They find that so many people seem to want to define them and others by various labels, be they community or otherwise, and they think that identity is both far more and far less complex than that. "I'm just me," they say, and want people to see who they truly are. Our workshop together was the first time they have written poetry, though they write a lot of prose, and it has inspired them to develop more such structures, including a variety of riddles. In the end, though, all they want is to be seen, and to shine a light on those who, like them, simply want to grow at their own pace.

PROSE

Alphabet Conversation

One of the entry activities we used during the prose workshops was writing a conversation in which each new piece of dialogue started with the next letter of the alphabet. One of my participants enjoyed this activity so much that they asked for their piece to be entered into the anthology.

Have a go at writing something similar yourself. It can be about anything, in any situation – as long as the first word of each new piece of dialogue starts with the next letter of the alphabet. Then read the piece below, comparing it to your own and absorbing the words on the page.

> *Alphabet Car Chase*
>
> "Ah, fucknuggets."
>
> "Blaine? What's up?", said the driver, flicking his eyes off the road.
>
> "Craps at six.", the robber said, already pulling out his gun to fire on the police cars racing up behind them.

3. CREATIVE WRITING PROJECT

"Delightful. Please hold for..." As they went screeching around the corner. "Ey, fuckhead, ya trying to get me to shoot meself?"

"'Fuckhead'? Really? I could always obey the traffic laws, Blaine, I'm sure they'd appreciate that." Said the driver, apparently more able to focus as much on sarcasm as the road as they roared past an extremely lucky pedestrian.

"God, you're a little shit." Blaine corrected his stance and moved back into position to fire at the encroaching police.

"Hold... still..." The bullet cracked out of the gun, but only found purchase in the siren.

"I see you've managed to improve the ambience."

Discussion

The author of this work felt that the piece was fun and enjoyed the freedom of unprompted writing while still having some guiding rule. Their first thought for 'A' was 'Ah' followed by a swearword, and they built an action scene from that, given that it implied some sort of problem.

This person has enjoyed being creative all their life, though mostly in a private and personal environment. They believe that "all the private stories and worlds I made or took part in were reflections of myself". In this manner, they feel that creativity enables you to interpret your identity, as you determine what still 'fits' and what does not.

Your Favourite Place on Campus

As well as exploring themes of identity, the project aimed to encourage my participants to discuss aspects of the student experience in their work, encouraging empathy in audiences by enabling their understanding that even while we often experience the world differently, we are all human and there are aspects of the student experience that we all understand.

If you are a student or teacher, think about your favourite place on campus at your university, college or school. If not, think back to your school or student days and see if you can recall a particular favourite place, or think of your favourite place at work or in some other communal space. Think about why you like it there, what it makes you feel, what you can see, hear, touch, smell or taste there. Spend some time writing a short description of that place, trying to capture the mood or sensation of being there through the words you use and the narrative you create.

Participant Responses

As you read, take some time to absorb the words on the page, and compare them to your own work, or to each other. Think about the diversity of experiences and meanings expressed throughout the pieces.

3. CREATIVE WRITING PROJECT

The Joyce Skinner Building

The corridors in the old building, the ones where you can feel like you can get lost, a labyrinth of knowledge and learning. Stumbling from one room to another, have I been here before? Does it matter?

The smell of old books and the creaking of steps, silence except these. At the weekend it is at rest, but in the week, it is a hive of activity, chatter, questions and discussions.

Forgetting where I am, I use the windows to help guide me, looking at the other buildings or the grass in front of Constance Stewart.

The place is not really one location, more a collection of spaces and rooms, but the steps and the small spaces and rooms provide a calming and reassuring space for my walk around.

School Butterflies

You hunker down behind the wall and try to catch your breath. They cannot see you here, cannot hear you, cannot find you.

Your back is pressed up firmly against the brick, scratchy in its solidarity, and a bead of sweat moves slowly down the side of your neck. You are not sure if they saw you, hope that they did not, but you've come here just in case.

The dirt beneath you is worn free of grass, the ground dry and dusty in the early June heat. You scuff your shoes as you lower yourself to sit cross legged, holding back a cough as the air is tainted for a moment.

You shudder as something tickles your arm, brush it off without much thought. The butterfly lands, stands dazed, and watches you for a moment. Some small part of you thinks about reaching out to stroke the butterfly's thin paper wings. Another, crueller, part considers crushing it beneath the sole of your shoe.

Before you can do either, the butterfly has taken off, lost in the blue expanse above you, leaving you blinking where you tried to follow its movements. Settling more comfortably against the wall, you wish

3. CREATIVE WRITING PROJECT

you'd thought to bring your book with you. You hadn't realised you would be bored when you had finished escaping. Instead, you think about the stories your mother used to tell you when you were small, try to remember the lessons she was trying to teach you. The ending escapes you and they always sounded better in her voice anyway, so you give up quickly.

Behind you, beyond the wall, the muffled sounds of other people reaches you for a moment, carried on the cool breeze. The wind doesn't extend to the bottom of the wall, rustling only the hair on the very top of your head, leaving the rest of you alone. You sink down further, tilt your body sideways until your ear is pressed to the dry ground, and try to get some sleep.

Disruption Does Not Exist

I snapped the sign from 'vacant' to 'occupied', hurrying in, and flicking the switch on to softly illuminate the quiet space. My eyes set their sights on the purple lived in the bean bag *[sic]* and fell into it, dropping my heavy bag and arms as a breath of relief or exhaustion escaped me. Wearily, my eyes shut while my hands reached down to the gentle carpet, spreading my fingers out to feel the fabric.

It is as though this room exists in its own space, in the labyrinth of the building. It is away from the world like a safe room in a videogame which shields me briefly from the maze of the outside where it overwhelms me, all while the maze insists that what it is, is normal. The outside here is muted, as though it had been sanded down to have no harsh edges, the outside in here barely enters, a light glows from a small window, but it does not take up space, the metallic cabinet behind sits behind me but also does not take up space, it sits against the pale-yellow walls that clasp around me. Whatever is outside, like noise, is snuffed out like the low murmurs outside are smoke from a blown-out candle.

Disruption does not exist as a concept here, it seems, it doesn't require anything from its visitors like an explanation as to why I am here or what could be overwhelming for me. It is just here in its own space.

3. CREATIVE WRITING PROJECT

A Peaceful Memory

There was a time in first year, when I sat next to the student's (sic) union gazing out at the small field. I spend a lot of time lurking there, having a cigarette, staring at my phone, sitting atop the picnic table rather than on the bench, but somehow, this one day in first year, it was the perfect break between winter and spring. I hadn't seen snow in years, and it was a blanket; I couldn't hear anything. The biggest tree stood bare, but not naked and scared like so many trees do, but with its own little white caps on each of its branches, and old nests from the seasons gone by sat quietly in the crooks. The sun was golden - I always loved winter sun, bright and welcoming, but not too warm – just reminding you that I am here, and I will rise another day. What was fascinating to me was the flowers gently poking their heads through; snowdrops and crocuses fighting to be heard through the all-encompassing silence, and the blossoming trees closer to the patio where I was. I've always loved cherry blossom, their recognition of how fleeting life can be, and how it welcomes the spring. Sakura never lasts too long – the trees bloom for maybe two weeks – but somehow, this year, it was brave enough to argue the cold and snow and start budding, pink against white against the gold of the sun. For a few moments, I was surrounded by my two favourite seasons simultaneously, and I was at peace. I don't recall where my mind went, or how long I stayed there. I never saw spring as nature fighting back against the winter, as I never saw winter as the death of the world. In some versions of the story, Persephone went willingly. There is a cycle. The snowdrops will always bloom, the cherry blossom will always die away, and the sun will always rise another day.

**

Discussion

For the first piece, the author selected as their favourite place an old building on campus called the Joyce Skinner Building, which has a somewhat maze-like interior, a tangle of interconnected passages and rooms. This person has loved this particular building for a number of years, describing an amazing maze that they found "unique and old". They no longer get a chance to visit it as much now, and it was the last place they went into on campus, so the space holds some good memories for them.

They find writing something that they really enjoy doing, though they mostly engage in nonfiction work. They describe the experience as "calming and intimate and just an amazing gift". They also write music and believe that this creative outlet allows them to express big things that they struggle to express verbally. They believe it releases their "more intense and in-depth and emotional communication".

3. CREATIVE WRITING PROJECT

They say that prior to the sessions, they found it difficult to get into writing creatively, but since the session together they have been writing about nature and starting to keep a more regular diary. They say that creativity is a huge part of their life, and that some of the most creative people they know are autistic. They enjoy being creative to express their emotions, cope with autistic burnout, anxiety and overwhelm, and challenge the stereotypes people often have about autism.

The author of the second piece chose to focus more on exploring their own creative abilities than expressing an explicit aspect of their experience. One of their biggest inspirations for this piece was the book *Human Acts* by Han Kang, which is partly written in second person. They do not attend campus often, so I suggested they focus on school instead. They do not believe that this piece is based on their own experience, and instead pictured the ending of primary school – the coarse, yellowing grass, worn by feet, and the idea of everyone having their own dens and spaces – and a tale flowed from that. They also didn't want to set it in a specific place, in order to give their readers freedom of imagination.

They do not usually write things quite so freeform, preferring to work on fanfiction or pieces inspired from other places. They found this exercise in original work interesting, and it inspired them to do it more. For them, writing comes in waves, and can be very useful as a stress-relief. They also often use fiction to put some of their emotional energy into a less destructive and more separated format. Finally, they often enjoy making references and including quotes, exploring pattern recognition and repeating phrases in different contexts, creating a sense of interconnection.

For the third piece, the author examined a safe space away from the expectations and stressors of the world, something that I am sure is a very relatable experience. At the time of writing this piece, this person was not doing too well with socialising and they often "feel like people struggle to understand what I mean". The space they wrote about is away from others, allowing a space where they do not have to think about that fact.

They use writing as a method to understand the world around them, and like to connect their writing to things that they are interested in. They say that they used it to "explore concepts outside of myself, so like what are other people doing, so it was me trying to figure out other people? And now it's me trying to figure out why I'm like this? Or sometimes to help, like, give comfort. 'Cause trying to look in and understand it, I find it to be a bit more comforting."

They find that they are better at expressing themselves through writing. They also enjoy using writing to express their emotions through metaphors, interpreting their emotional truth rather than a literal expression of the situation. They believe that creativity allows them to give themselves respect, understanding and validation, and they sometimes use it to communicate with their inner child and give their past self more understanding, particularly relating to autism. They also think that creativity allows for the exploration of the differences and similarities between people, because people can write different things about the same stimuli. For example, "how many love songs are there?!"

Finally, the author of the fourth piece drew on memory rather than location. They decided to write about one of their favourite memories from their first year on campus. This moment also holds a special place in their heart as it was the first time they had seen snow in seven years, and snow is one of their favourite things. They enjoy the colours and environments of the colder months, and they love how quiet it gets when it snows.

The author of this piece felt that the project helped to draw them out of the dry spell they had been in with writing and appreciated the community the group built up. Writing is so often a solitary hobby, and listening to and talking to others helped them feel more confident in their writing and more comfortable sharing it.

A Conversation with your Younger Self

It is well-researched and well-evidenced that creative writing can be a cathartic and enlightening experience[68]. In many of my own participatory sessions in applied drama and arts we

---

[68] Deveney, C., & Lawson, P. (2022). Writing your way to well-being: An IPA analysis of the therapeutic effects of creative writing on mental health and the processing of emotional difficulties. Counselling and Psychotherapy Research, 22(2), 292–300. https://doi.org/10.1002/capr.12435

have been encouraged to communicate with our younger selves, and this has always been an important and engaging activity for me. Many autistic people carry unpleasant experiences from their childhood which still impact them as they get older, and the prevalence of mental health issues in autistic people is noticeable. While this project did not intend to target therapeutic aims, the applied arts often give an access point to therapeutic experiences, and prompts like this help to access that sense of self-identity and self-love.

Think about what you might like to say to your younger self. Have a go at writing a short conversation between yourself and them, considering both perspectives on the conversation. This can be structured as prose or script. Don't be surprised or concerned if this feels very impactful or targets deeper emotions than you expect; but equally, don't be concerned if it feels very surface-level for you.

Participant Responses

As you read, take some time to absorb the words on the page, and compare them to your own work, or to each other. Think about the diversity of experiences and meanings expressed throughout the pieces.

3. CREATIVE WRITING PROJECT

You're So Tall!

"Woah." The little girl widened her eyes. "You're so tall!"

I laughed. "Thank you. Would you like to be tall, too?"

"Yeah!" The girl grinned. My eyes alight on the natural gap between her two front teeth, and instinctively I feel the false one at the front of my own mouth ruefully. "One day, I'm going to be taller than my dad!"

"Well, I have a secret to tell you." I smiled and leant down to whisper in her ear. She practically broke my nose bouncing up in her excitement. "I am you. From the future."

She looked at me in awe. "Really?!" I nodded, and then she frowned. "You don't look like me. I want to have long princess hair. All the way down to my waist."

"I know. I remember." I smiled, melancholy, and sat cross-legged on the grass beside her, running my hands over the cool blades. "But things change. Lots of things. Look--" And I launched into an explanation of one of the stories she told herself. The ones she didn't tell anyone.

Satisfied that I was who I said, she sat slowly next to me, and I could feel her confusion because it was my own. "You look sad."

"I'm not sad. I'm--" I paused, trying to find the right words. "I miss you."

"What do you mean?"

"Never mind." I sighed, before turning to her with a smile. "You know you're awesome, right?"

"Yeah." She nodded, casually, drawing with a stick in the dirt.

"I mean it."

"So do I." She smiled up at me. But then it faltered, just for a moment. "I'm different, though, aren't I? Does that change?"

"No." I smiled. "But we understand it more now. And it's not something you can or should try to change."

"Okay." She nodded. We were quiet for a bit. "Why are you here?"

"I wanted to see you. To tell you how much I love you. Your passion and energy and creativity—"

"We haven't lost that, have we?" She demanded, over-serious, frowning into my eyes.

"No. But it-- it comes and goes. Everything is so much more tiring."

"You sound like mum."

3. CREATIVE WRITING PROJECT

"Ugh." I shoved her in the arm, lightly. "Don't say that."

There was a silence. My traveller's watch beeped. I wanted to say more, but I didn't want to change her decisions.

SCRIPT

A Conversation with Your Younger Self (Continued)
Click the Mouse and the Future Changes

YOUNGER is sitting on her own. She doesn't look any different age wise to OLDER, but the burden of a difficult year shows in the sadness of OLDER's eyes. There are voices overlay? [sic] *In the background of YOUNGER's room, but they sound more like distant memories. People who told her negative things, that she could not do something she did not deserve something, YOUNGER is looking at a laptop and an extra screen, one screen contains an application form for a university, the other is an application for a postgraduate degree in SENDi. She takes a breath and coughs out a deep sigh. Her face is pale. OLDER appears next to her and looks around the room. The voices fade out as the OLDER appears.*

OLDER: In a couple of days, you are going to get told to tidy this.

YOUNGER jumps in shock and looks up to the near identical version of herself, then at the slightly messy room, with a sudden realisation, that it is slightly messy.

OLDER: Some moments in life define us. This is one of them. You feel like you can't make a choice, because either way, something is going to go wrong. You are going to upset someone, you are going to make a mistake, you are going to hurt someone. But honestly, you will no matter which way you choose. And at least this is a choice. There is a time, where you will feel you have limited choices, or no choices at all. *[She stops abruptly.]*

YOUNGER: What do you mean?

OLDER: I can't tell you, because if I did, it would mean that I have never told you. The future works in strange ways.

YOUNGER: *[nods in understanding because they both have the same thought process and understand each other when nobody else does, so that sentence that will make absolutely no sense to anyone but her, makes sense to the older version of her. Just like this one.]* What do I decide?

OLDER: That's up to you. You have always told yourself to follow your heart, but we get caught up in making others happy, that we don't know how to be happy ourselves. You don't want to pick because you can't try them. But I have. I have made that choice

3. CREATIVE WRITING PROJECT

that you are sitting there telling yourself off for. I tried one of the options. And now I am trying the other. You are me, so I know which one you will pick unless I intervene now. If you choose now, to change your mind, to click the other button, to make a choice, it can change your future.

Both repeat at exactly the same time: "turn the wheel and the future changes" a quote from their still favourite tv show on Netflix.

YOUNGER: That's what I'm worried about.

OLDER: *[nods in sympathy]* I know. But not making a choice, is making a choice in itself.

YOUNGER: What did you choose?

OLDER: The more difficult option. *[She didn't need to gesture to the screen, because YOUNGER knows exactly what the more difficult option is.]*

YOUNGER: Really? Why?

OLDER: You are me. You know why.

They both nod at the same time.

YOUNGER: I really am afraid

OLDER: I know. I was too. But I need to tell you that this is for you. Not for what everyone else wants you to do. And I can't grasp that idea either, still can't. And you know in your heart of hearts what option is right for you. What you have always wanted to do, you just rejected the idea because people told you that you couldn't, that you weren't worthy of it. That you wouldn't be good enough at it. I won't tell you that you will be amazing, but you will learn and find parts of yourself, that you didn't know you had"

YOUNGER: Click with me?

OLDER knows exactly what YOUNGER is going to decide. She smiles, and looks around the room for one last time, her hand lands next to YOUNGER's on the mousepad. They click send together, and the application for working in a special needs school was sent off. OLDER fades away, as YOUNGER's future changes. This conversation never happened. Because YOUNGER clicked a button. And her whole future, it changed. But somehow, the warmth of her older self's hand lingers for a little while longer.

Discussion

One of the first things people comment on when they meet or see the author of the first piece is 'you're so tall' or 'you've grown so much', and that is one of their favourite things because as a child, they always wanted to outgrow their dad, who is very tall. They have not quite achieved that goal, but they are very close!

When seeing this prompt, this person was struck by how much has changed and yet how much has stayed the same for them.

3. CREATIVE WRITING PROJECT

So many of their dreams and so much of their personality remains, but in their opinion, "adulthood makes everything so much harder. I feel tired all the time, because I have to do everything myself, and support is so hard to access and so rarely useful". They were also struck by how little they would wish to tell their younger self, even about being autistic, which is something they found out post-early-childhood, because their decisions have made them who they are, and they do not regret the lessons they have learned or the person they have become.

Decisions, choices, lessons and becoming do not stop after childhood, however. The author of the third piece wanted to look to the past as a metaphor for the present. At the time of writing, they "had a difficult choice to make, as shown by the two options on the computer screen and I was feeling like I didn't know what to do about it".

Through this piece, they began to explore some of their deepest insecurities: from wanting to be happy, to not wanting anything to go wrong, to being scared of "something I recently had to do, something that I had a very limited choice in, to protect the people I care about". They also said that "this writing helped me to make the choice that I was struggling with".

I think you will agree that their honesty is invaluable and inspiring, and their work reflects the difficult choices we as humans so often have to make about who to please and how, and brings out the reflective, gentle melancholy we so often experience when looking back at difficult choices from the past while thinking of how to make present ones.

A Conversation Between a Modern-Day Antagonist and Protagonist

Many of the stories we see or read feature conflict, and it has been said that you cannot have a story without it. Whether that is true or not, many of us will be familiar with the concept of protagonists and antagonists – the former being the often (though not always) good force or person within the story that the audience follows and usually supports, and the latter being the force or person causing or presenting difficulties to them achieving their goals. Real life is not always so cut and dry, although most people would consider themselves the protagonists of their own story. Some stories try to bring this complexity out through their narrative, making use of what is often known as 'grey morality' – where characters or forces make decisions for reasons and with consequences that are neither good nor bad, and have complex and interesting motivations for those decisions.

Think about where you might set a conversation between an antagonist and a protagonist in the modern day and have a go at writing it without considering complexity. Who would be the villain and why? How would you present the two people or forces? Then try to edit or rewrite the conversation to craft more complex characters, with different motivations and a little more humanity.

3. CREATIVE WRITING PROJECT

Participant Responses

As you read the participants' responses overleaf, take some time to absorb the words on the page, and compare them to your own work. Think about the diversity of experiences and meanings expressed throughout the pieces.

Goodbye, Johnson

Johnson: You wanted to see me sir?

Wilson: *[Sighs.]* Yes. Well, actually, I don't in particular, but I rather have to here.

J: Sir?

W: I hate to say this but... you're fired.

There is a moment of quiet

J: ...What?

W: Upper management's decision. 'Cull workforce by 10%'. We only have ten people here. You're the unlucky one.

J: But... but why? We've had record profits this quarter - and the last! We just got that new project out.

W: Yes, we did, and apparently corporate thinks that makes it a good time to do layoffs, so they get a bigger cut.

There is a much longer pause.

J: but... that's not fair.

W: *[tired]* I know it isn't Johnson. But that's it. Corporate has made the decision, and my job is to inform you of it.

J: Why me?

W: To be honest? I removed Thompson and Jason because... well, Thompson's our best and Jason's got his new kid. And then... I picked at random.

J: *[pleading voice]* Sir, come on. Please. There's got to be something you can do. I need this job.

W: I know, Johnson, but so do I. So does everyone else in the department. If I don't comply, it's my position, and then it's all of theirs when whoever replaces me messes everything up. I can't do that to them.

J: *[visibly angry]* but you can do it to me, right?

W: ... I suppose I can. Because I am. Johnson –

J: *[furious]* Fuck you. FUCK YOU. You're a bastard, and I hope you die.

He walks out the office and slams the door.

W: ...Goodbye, Johnson.

Discussion

Only 22% of autistic people are in any kind of employment, according to the Office for National Statistics. Autistic people have one of the worst employment rates; compare the aforementioned statistic to the fact that around 50% of disabled people are in work, or just over 80% of non-disabled people. In addition, around 75% of autistic people live with their parents, compared to 16% of disabled people generally.[69] And it is well-known that mental health issues occur far more frequently in neurodivergent people than neurotypical people.

This inspires very real fears in many neurodivergent individuals of being unable to find work or become an active member of society, and these fears are a large part of the inspiration behind this person's piece. They also discussed the general fears of their generation regarding large companies and their unfeeling attitudes.

The initial piece featured a much less sympathetic character in Wilson, and when they began to consider the editing prompt, they were inspired to develop the piece to humanise him. They said that this "forced them to confront this fear directly" and they decided to "put [Wilson] too enmeshed and crushed in the cogs of the soulless profit machine, and reframed them to somebody having to make a sacrifice for the good of the rest".

The Opening Scene of a Movie About Your Life, or that of Your Childhood Best Friend

Screenplays and scriptwriting share a number of often unexpected similarities with writing prose or poetry, with a distinction which can often be used to define many of the differences between the two. Not all, of course, but keeping this

---

[69] New shocking data highlights the autism employment gap. (n.d.). Retrieved 28 September 2023, from https://www.autism.org.uk/what-we-do/news/new-data-on-the-autism-employment-gap

3. CREATIVE WRITING PROJECT

in mind is often useful. A screenplay or script provides guidance for the actors, designers and directors, rather than creating a visual world for the audience. There is less concern regarding overexplaining in description, and less importance on creating mood with language, but description and image craft can still be important.

Consider what the opening scene of a movie about your life or that of your childhood best friend would look like. You can give it a genre, if you so choose, or work without that in mind. Try to write the shape of the opening scene – what would we see or hear, what dialogue would be spoken, how would the audience be introduced to our characters or locations. Have a go at writing the scene.

Participant Responses

As you read, take some time to absorb the words on the page, and compare them to your own work. Think about the diversity of experiences and meanings expressed throughout the pieces.

The Love that Moves the Sun and Other Stars

Paige's room, the forbidden library.

Paige is absentmindedly stroking Dewey, the library cat. Her other hand is gently touching the pages of a book, fingers softly brushing over a few passages. One in particular catches her attention.

Pov: looking directly at the pages of the book, the words seem to glow in a golden colour. "L'amor che move il sole e l'altre stelle" The love that moves the sun and the other stars.

Paige: *[to Dewey, sad voice]* Do you ever think that someday we would be able to see, the love, the sun and the stars?

Dewey: *[Miaows a few times.]*

Paige: v/o- (Translation – we already have love, we have each other).

Paige gets up from the floor and gently places the book, that is written entirely in Italian, down. One of her favourites. She goes over to the cold stone wall of the library that she has never been allowed to leave and opens the thick curtains, just so she can see, for a small second, the world outside. It is a cloudy day but that does not make the sky any less beautiful and any less forbidden.

3. CREATIVE WRITING PROJECT

And of course, there is the dragon that created the little flames that always seemed to rest as smoke along the clouds. The dragon does not let anyone out of the library, other than by the means of learning knowledge from books. Of course, you could always escape into a different world through a book.

Pov- we see a combination of Paige's sad face and a large green dragon in the courtyard.

Paige: *[sighs and draws back the curtain.]* We do. We have each other, and we have these books.

Her elbows are placed as she starts to sing as she does every day to the sky outside, her voice as beautiful as every bird that passes in the early mornings. But the difference today, is that it is not the early morning, and her song was not drowned out by the birds, or the insects, or the early morning roaring of the dragon. It was a song of hope, of peace, of a child who learned about the world, but is not of the world.

Discussion

When this person sat down to write this piece, they were feeling down about their life and not up to writing about themselves, and they could not recall having a particular childhood friend. This person, like many of my participants, utilised the role-playing game Dungeons and Dragons as a creative outlet, hobby and coping strategy. They therefore decided to use one of their characters from the game as their inspiration for this piece.

They discussed how many people they know, including themselves, would "love to be stuck in a magical library, with all the knowledge possible, but Paige wants to actually see the world for herself, to be a part of it, instead of separate from it". Paige's story leads her out of the library to a group of friends, but for many autistic people, that sensation of being "a child who learned about the world, but is not of the world" remains true for much of their lives. The author of this piece consistently discussed how that was one of her favourite quotes, and it is not hard to see that expressing one's own experience through the creative interpretations of fiction is something that autistic people are very capable of doing, and enjoy doing very much.

**

3. CREATIVE WRITING PROJECT

Summary of Findings

In this chapter, a broad range of examples of autistic-written literature have been reproduced, and you have been offered the chance to engage in some writing yourself. Through these works, we have discovered:

- Contrary to what is often posited, autistic people can and do understand metaphor and non-literal language and are often highly creative with their language use and meaning making.
- Creative writing enables people (including, and perhaps especially, autistic people) to express emotions and experiences which they would not otherwise be able to articulate. Using language, specifically, also presents limitations, and it can be enjoyable to play with those limits.
- Inspiration comes from many places, including life experiences, identity and culture.
- Sensory overload can cause a physical reaction, and language can help to express such experiences.
- Autistic experiences are diverse and varied, and many people just want to be seen.
- Creativity is fun and can be freeing.
- Writing can provide a space to release your emotions in a safer and more productive manner.
- It can also help with introspection, allowing one to explore different aspects of one's identity.
- Writing in a group in which discussions and sharing can

be accessed can increase confidence and expression.
- Making use of large-scale metaphors can assist in decision making and understanding of life situations.
- Autistic people often experience fears about employment, and employment rates for autistic people are low.
- In the words of one of my participants, "I'm just me." Though we may experience similar things or have some differences, the same is true of autistic and non-autistic people: we are all just us.

Issues with the approach

While it is true that creative writing does not require verbal communication, thus enabling those who utilise typed or written forms of communication to engage with the work, this project still presents some limitations. There are autistic people who struggle to use words in any format to communicate what they mean, a challenge which can be exacerbated by common comorbidities. Additionally, even for those who commonly use written or spoken language, playing with it and using it creatively can still be a challenging activity. Struggles with spelling and grammar, difficulty translating what is meant into words, challenges understanding the tasks and indeed unrelated struggles such as multilingualism, can all present barriers to engagement with projects like this.

In future, making use of alternative methods of creative engagement, such as music, dance or visual arts could enhance the project further, allowing access for those who struggle

3. CREATIVE WRITING PROJECT

to or simply do not wish to use words. Opportunity for such engagement is ripe, and it is my hope to develop the project further, allowing for such engagement and carrying this creative impact to even more diverse communities.

**

CHAPTER 4

What has emerged from these projects?

In this final chapter we consider what may have emerged from these projects and what they might suggest about lived experience of autism. How are these experiences supported by the wider literature on the subject, and in what ways might these perspectives augment or challenge these received wisdoms? What avenues for further research into living as an autistic person do these projects suggest and what do the successes or otherwise of the methods employed here tell us about means of exploration going forward?

For many years we have been told of the 'heterogeneity of autism presentation'[70]: if you have met one autistic person, we are reminded, you have met just one autistic person, and we know that autism presents in different people in different ways.

---

[70] See for example, Masi, A., DeMayo, M. M., Glozier, N., & Guastella, A. J. (2017). An overview of autism spectrum disorder, heterogeneity and treatment options. Neuroscience bulletin, 33, 183-193.

I am not sure why this might be surprising. After all, if you have met one person, you have met one person, and you would not necessarily expect that person to be particularly like anyone else. If Autistic people are viewed as people, then of course each is different. Why wouldn't we be?

What is being suggested, of course, is that the way that the autism manifests itself is very different across different autistic people, and for a medical profession keen to 'quantify' autism, this has been very frustrating. Observing how autism appears from the outside, usually through behaviour and often in children, means that those seeking classification have had a difficult time of it. It is not surprising that the diagnostic criteria for autism remain the subject of some debate[71].

(It is interesting, as an aside, that it is often proposed as an element of autism that autistic people have a preference for systemising, classifying, quantifying and identifying, yet it is the external medical community, not those who are autistic, who are providing the driving force in this endeavour.)

It is important to note that, even as we understand that all autistic people are different and that categorising a list of behaviours that define the difference between an autistic

---

[71] For example, Volkmar, F. R., Reichow, B., & McPartland, J. (2022). Classification of autism and related conditions: progress, challenges, and opportunities. Dialogues in clinical neuroscience; Waterhouse, L. (2022). Heterogeneity thwarts autism explanatory power: A proposal for endophenotypes. Frontiers in Psychiatry, 13, 947653.

4. WHAT HAS EMERGED FROM THESE PROJECTS?

person and someone who is not is a challenge, this does not mean that we agree with the sentiment that 'everyone is a little bit autistic'[72]. Autism, in all its wonder, difference and variety, remains disabling life experience in the world in which we live. If everyone were autistic, every space would be designed to accommodate for painful sensory stimuli, everyone would be accommodating for a diverse array of stims and social behaviours, and there would be no need for such things as 'masking' or the 'double empathy problem'.

Indeed, this sensation that there is categorically something different about the way autistic people experience the world when compared to their neurotypical peers is expressed in both projects. The description of being "a part, apart" from the daffodils (and their metaphorical reflection, the activities of neurotypical people) 'marries' beautifully with the idea expressed in the final piece of the anthology of being someone who "learned about the world, but is not of the world". In both groups, these ideas were agreed upon and supported.

What remains unclear in all of this is whether or not there may be a greater homogeneity for autistic people in the experience (as opposed to the presentation) of autism. Autism may look different in how it influences behaviours that are observable by an external observer, but what are the commonalities to the experience of being autistic from the inside? This has been the

---

[72] See, for example, https://www.forbes.com/sites/drnancydoyle/021/01/16/is-everyone-a-little-autistic/; Beardon, L. (2017). Autism and Asperger syndrome in adults. Hachette UK, p.13.

thrust of much Social Model research into autism in recent years, and through this research by and with the autistic community, what autism 'is' is gradually becoming clearer.

Yet as we discussed in the introduction to this book, it can be a challenge for autistic people to describe differences of experience when those differences are, for that person, the norm. The creative approaches discussed in this book have been an exploration of how using ideas expressed in created writing may be a way through this conundrum. Creativity is highly personal and, by its nature, formative (in creating, whether text or meaning from text, you are bringing about something new – generating, developing, forming an original product – and that 'something' may well have a powerful reflection back onto the creator). So, have there been commonalities in what the creators in the reading and writing projects explored in this book have articulated?

One thing is, I think, very clear. The argument that all autistic people (because of their autism) struggle with non-literal, figurative or metaphorical concepts can be firmly put aside. There is tremendous enjoyment of the exploration of language evident across these examples, with participants exhibiting often highly creative, playful and exciting responses. We know that autistic enthusiasm for the world is mirrored in – and may perhaps sometimes be accessed through – reading[73].

---

[73] See, for example, Chapple, M., Williams, S., Billington, J., Davis, P., & Corcoran, R. (2021). An analysis of the reading habits of autistic adults compared to neurotypical adults and implications for future

4. WHAT HAS EMERGED FROM THESE PROJECTS?

The teachers in chapter one report exploring nuanced social interactions and conventions through following characters as presented in stories; the concepts and complexities of 'dialogue' may be so much easier to follow for us all when written down. The outdated concept of 'mindblindness' in autism[74] led many in the past to wrongly attribute autistic people with being deficient in the understanding of the thoughts and feelings of others. What is clear in the richness shared in these projects is that autistic people, just like anyone else, may be fascinated by the inner lives of others and can skilfully relate others' worlds to their own. Using words is a powerful tool for us all to both consider and share these explorations. There is, additionally, an originality to much of the interpretation seen here as shared by autistic voices, and a spontaneity and rich exploration of both the content of what is being discussed and the language used to do so. The perception of Wordsworth's cloud as being a metaphor for autistic 'alone-ness', of his host of daffodils as a potential analogy for togetherness and separation, of a Rubik's cube to represent the almost infinite variety and beauty of something 'unsolved', each of these examples show a sophisticated consideration of abstract notions through concrete examination. And in creating metaphor and figurative language themselves (externally from interpreting something already present), autistic people also show notable creativity and diversity. Examples include using the imagery of autumn

---

interventions. Research in Developmental Disabilities, 115, 104003.

[74] Baron-Cohen, S. (1997). Mindblindness: An essay on autism and theory of mind. MIT press.

leaves left on the ground to reflect the dichotomies of life, exploring sensory overload through a diverse array of images and metaphors, using colour to interpret one's identity, using imagery, mythological inspiration and a variety of metaphors and similes to explore experiences of peace and hope, and many more examples than we can fit into this list. We would recommend going back over the anthology in Chapter 3 and highlighting all the metaphorical or figurative descriptions and language choices, but are pretty sure that in doing so, you will highlight most of the work!

Some commonality of themes across these explorations does also emerge. One, sadly, is that of insecurity and lack of confidence – both of the participants' ability to initially approach the tasks, and then, through the tasks, of the wider world. Those taking part in the Shared Reading project showed a universal mistrust in their ability to interpret poetry which says little for our current education system. The participants needed considerable encouragement before gradually being able to bring forth the wealth of interpretations that they brought to the task. This lack of confidence is exhibited in many aspects of what these discussions then explore. While this concern over ability at poetry analysis is not exclusive to the autistic experience[75] and nor, perhaps, are some of the anxieties expressed, it is important to note how much these

---

[75] Hawkins, L. K., & Certo, J. L. (2014). It's something that I feel like writing, instead of writing because I'm being told to: Elementary boys' experiences writing and performing poetry. Pedagogies: An International Journal, 9(3), 196–215. https://doi.org/10.1080/1554480X.2014.921857

4. WHAT HAS EMERGED FROM THESE PROJECTS?

anxieties are universally expressed. You do not need to have an autistic person's pattern recognition to understand the links that therefore must be made.

These anxieties concern a variety of aspects of life, though perhaps one of the most notable concerns was expressed regarding employment. The employment gap between autistic and non-autistic people (and, as a note, disabled and non-disabled people) remains shocking and disturbing, and it is clearly an issue which must be voiced, accepted and tackled. This disparity, counter-intuitively, may be the most stark in autistic graduates[76]. There are many possible reasons for this (the inaccessibility of interview processes, workplaces, and working hours, to name just a few), but small alterations could change this for the better, and the more autistic people are in work, the more diverse, accessible and understanding our workplaces will become.

It is interesting in this to note how accessible and safe our participants felt the projects to be. Not only does this imply that spaces curated by autistic people are, unsurprisingly, generally better for autistic people, but also that there is perhaps something to be said about the accessibility inherent in creativity. It may be easier to curate one's level of engagement in a creative space, and it does not take much searching to find

---

[76] Pesonen, H. V., Tuononen, T., Fabri, M., & Lahdelma, M. (2022). Autistic graduates: graduate capital and employability. Journal of education and work, 35(4), 374-389.

a host of autistic people thriving in creative employment[77]. There is rich potential for further exploration of how and why creative employment in and of itself works (and doesn't!) for the autistic experience.

Additionally, a number of concerns over identity and the 'mask' were expressed. These included the hiding of repetitive movements so as not to stand out, being an odd-one-out on the outskirts of a crowd, ideas of being altered or 'smoothed', rejecting the identity of 'the reliable one', aligning identity with colour and exploring the concept of identity through labelling. It is clear that the autistic participants in these projects have a rich and diverse understanding of identity and self, as well as a genuine interest in exploring it. It is also clear that intrinsic to the autistic experience may be a sensation of being forced to hide one's true self, often at great cost. This uncertainty and anxiety around expressing oneself is one of the things that we aimed to tackle through these projects, by allowing autistic people (including ourselves) a space to be their authentic selves.

It might have been predicted that some of the aforementioned fears and doubts would be compounded by sensory issues. Sensory differences are some of the most strongly investigated

---

[77] E.g. Books by Actually Autistic Authors (353 books). (n.d.). Retrieved 2 December 2023, from https://www.goodreads.com/list/show/113806. Books_by_Actually_Autistic_Authors, or Famous People with Autism [180+ Athletes, Actors, Musicians & More!] | Ongig Blog. (n.d.). Retrieved 2 December 2023, from https://blog.ongig.com/diversity-and-inclusion/famous-people-with-autism/.

4. WHAT HAS EMERGED FROM THESE PROJECTS?

elements of autism, and there is general agreement that one element of being autistic may be a difference in the way that sensory data is processed and perceived by the individual.[78] This may result in profoundly enhanced sensory feedback (across any or all of the senses) or, indeed, may produce a reduced perception of some sensory messages. Although these less usual experiences may result in considerable distress for many autistic people, and indeed, there are clear examples of this discussed in the pieces produced in the anthology, the participants in these projects also reported more positive experiences, such as explorations of colour interpretation, and discussion of the sensory reasons for spaces, objects and food to be safe or enjoyable.

The exploration of differences in colour perception as discussed in Chapter Two were exciting, and in chapter three, we saw participants taking this further by interpreting identity, self-understanding and their needs through the medium of colour. It is also interesting to note that one participant highlighted a "colour changing light" as an important sensory experience for them when struggling and dealing with burnout, and that the pleasing nature of the Rubik's cube when the colours are intermingled was highlighted. It seems clear that colour perception and interpretation is often an important part of the autistic experience, whatever that experience leads to.

---

[78] For example, Kirby, A. V., Bilder, D. A., Wiggins, L. D., Hughes, M. M., Davis, J., Hall-Lande, J. A., ... & Bakian, A. V. (2022). Sensory features in autism: Findings from a large population-based surveillance system. Autism Research, 15(4), 751-760.

The richness of sensory experiences more widely was articulately explored – participants shared some of the detail of their visual perceptions, of the importance of comfortable clothing, of the richness of smells and tastes and of the physical sensation of some foods in the mouth. Additionally, many of the places identified as 'favourite places' were described as such due to the presence or lack of a variety of sensory stimuli – the quietness, the smell of old books, the physical space, a bean bag, a light, the feeling of the carpet, the sight of a cherry tree, and much more. Throughout the anthology, the senses are often used to bring a richer understanding of the way autistic people live their lives and interpret the world. When we adapted this into performance, we worked to give the audience a sensation of the experience, in order to immerse them into the writing. It was important to the group that the scenes were underscored by music or sound effects and that projection and images were used to grant a deeper understanding of the experiences being expressed.

The strong impression from these projects is that sensory differences need not be distressing if they can be mediated by the person experiencing them. The option to escape from sensations when they overwhelm seems, when present, to allow for the enjoyment of those same sensations within a safe context. As usual, it is not the 'being autistic' that seems to create a problem, but the fact of having to manage that autism in a neurotypical world. Further, this striving to merely 'manage' may block much of what is enhancing in autistic experience for that individual when co-existing in the neurotypical plane. When

4. WHAT HAS EMERGED FROM THESE PROJECTS?

we consider the idea that many autistic people are constantly self-regulating, managing their interaction with the stimuli around them, and attempting to function healthily within that by themselves, we begin to understand why one of the most universal experiences in autism is exhaustion. As one participant said, "we have like three full-time brain jobs up there and only one brain to do it, and most of the advice out there is for people who only have one full-time brain job and one equivalent brain." Creating accessible spaces for autistic people means creating spaces where they no longer have to do the mental work of self-regulation and management, or creating space where they can do that safely rather than in-the-moment – which removes one of those "brain jobs" and allows more mental space for enjoyment and engagement in the world.

The joys of (mediated) sensory experiences were just some of the pleasures and enthusiasms around being autistic that emerged from these projects. Participants affirmed their delight in monologuing, in sharing what interests them in a one-sided conversation. There was playfulness here, and recognition that although this might be unsatisfactory for the listener, the monologuer gains hugely from it and – what is more – does not care about the sensitivities of the listener! It is interesting that, in many ways, creative writing might be described as a more socially acceptable version of this activity. Perhaps the listener (or, in this case, reader) feels more autonomous about their level of engagement with the monologue; and perhaps we should bring some sense of that autonomy into our interactions with autistic people. Some of the wonder that attention to detail and noticing through strong focus can bring was shared, and it was challenged why this might ever be seen as a deficit. This monotropic focus emerged in these discussions as a strength and a delight of autism. There were many, many examples to emerge in these projects of positive aspects to being autistic, and participants seemed happy to have an opportunity to give voice to these experiences that counter the purely deficit descriptors of who they are.

This opportunity, through participation in these reading and writing creative groups, gives rise to further considerations. Much of what was said points to the act of taking part having a positive impact on the experiences being discussed. The very opportunity to take part in these discussions around the lived experience of being autistic within autistic spaces seems to have resulted in some feelings of freedom and exhilaration. The participants enjoyed themselves. What is more, the use of language as explored here seems to have provided a vehicle for regulation of some of the aspects that are otherwise difficult. Many participants discussed being overwhelmed, of experiencing sensory or mental overload in various aspects of their lives, and the opportunity for exploration of these challenges through these creative approaches seems to have been positive for them. It is often stated amongst writing circles that writing is a solitary hobby, and engaging in these projects also encouraged our participants to practise similar activities with more regularity and focus. Additionally, when asked to discuss what writing or creativity meant to them, the vast majority of participants discussed using it as a form of emotional regulation and release.

4. WHAT HAS EMERGED FROM THESE PROJECTS?

Using metaphors, exploring figurative and non-literal language, seems to have at times 'unlocked' areas of expression that were otherwise difficult for people to access. The projects appear to have provided opportunities in which to explore emotions and experiences in a productive and secure environment. The idea of using creative writing, words and creative play as a tool for emotional exploration is not a new one.[79] However, the obvious use of metaphor and non-literal language has often limited its exploration with autistic people. It is interesting to note that the use of fictional scenarios and performance-based techniques has been used (and often abused) with autistic people for some time – why has it been assumed, then, that we would not be able to comprehend fiction in the written word? In any case, the combination of knowing what to articulate (through the structures of the reading and writing tasks) and having vehicles with which to articulate these ideas (through the activities taking place and the figurative approaches being explored) seems to have been a powerful one.

Further, the sense of community, and most notably (and joyfully), intersectional community expressed by those taking part in these projects is important. These have been recorded through much of what has emerged; the power of shared world-building, for example, and of the creation of rich social

---

[79] e.g. Deveney, C., & Lawson, P. (2022). Writing your way to well-being: An IPA analysis of the therapeutic effects of creative writing on mental health and the processing of emotional difficulties. Counselling and Psychotherapy Research, 22(2), 292–300. https://doi.org/10.1002/capr.12435 or Roy *, E., Casanova, M. F.,

networks of autistic people working together has been an important element of these projects. There seems throughout to have been an understanding that exploring different aspects of autistic identity through social discussion provides enhancement above and beyond what is experienced alone. Every autistic person is different; every autistic person is themself, but introspection can be isolating, and realisation that others are sharing elements of your journey can be liberating. Additionally, discussing differences in journeys, behaviours and experiences reinforces the rejection of stereotypes (...and can cause some hilarity!). Behaviours that are masked in other contexts can be unpacked and considered, stereotypes can be critiqued and the challenges of overcoming the 'double empathy' barrier between neurotypical and neurodivergent people can be considered within the safe space of fellowship. There is great beauty in the diversity of autistic presentation, fascination in the diversity of autistic experience, but perhaps also some considerable reassurance in the similarity of a shared world.

This latter approach supports the growing concept of autistic culture, where shared community experiences can support individual identities within a concept of 'being autistic' that is accepted by that community. This concept suggests a group dynamic of shared experiences, not observable criteria[80]. The growing field of Critical Autism Studies is an interdisciplinary research approach, led by autistic people, which challenges

---

[80] Farahar, C. (2022). Chapter 19: Autistic identity, culture, community, and space for well-being. The Routledge International Handbook of Critical Autism Studies.

4. WHAT HAS EMERGED FROM THESE PROJECTS?

the deficit model of autism and seeks to give autistic voices platform, respect and credibility.

Within the small projects discussed in this book, these voices have been firmly foregrounded. All elements in the book have emerged from within the autistic community itself so that this book on 'creativity in autism' is, we hope, an act of creativity in itself. Helen Kara[81], who wrote the foreword for this book and who is a lead proponent of creative research methodologies, discusses the overlap between arts-based activities and creative research methods, suggesting that '[r]esearch is a fundamental part of arts' (p.29) and citing its place in fiction writing[82], creative nonfiction writing[83] and poetry[84]. We research to create, and we create through research. These projects articulate ways that the 'voice' of autistic people may be better heard, in research and in society. They are creative approaches and create through the approaches undertaken.

They are also fun! In being ready to explore autistic communication, this book has used that created communication exploratively, to play with and enjoy the very elements being

---

[81] Kara, H. (2020). Creative Research Methods 2e: A Practical Guide. Policy Press.

[82] Spencer, K. (2013). New modes of creative writing research. Research methods in creative writing, 78-101.

[83] Brien, D. L. (2013). Non-fiction writing research. Research methods in creative writing, 34-55.

[84] Lasky, K. (2013). Poetics and creative writing research. Research methods in creative writing, 14-33.

explored. We have very much enjoyed making it and taking part in the projects discussed, and we hope that this positive approach to exploring autism – the enjoyment, playfulness and spirit of adventure reported here – extends to you who read it.

**